Education, Democracy, and the Moral Life

Michael S. Katz, Ph.D. • Susan Verducci, Ph.D.
Gert Biesta, Ph.D.
Editors

Education, Democracy, and the Moral Life

 Springer

Editors
Michael S. Katz, Ph.D.
San Jose State University
One Washington Square,
San Jose, CA 95192-0077,
USA

Susan Verducci, Ph.D.
San Jose State University
One Washington Square,
San Jose, CA 95192-0092,
USA

Gert Biesta, Ph.D.
Institute of Education,
University of Stirling,
Stirling, FK9 4LA

ISBN: 978-90-481-2355-1 (PB)
ISBN: 978-1-4020-8625-0 (HB)
e-ISBN: 978-1-4020-8626-7

Library of Congress Control Number: 2009922355

Printed on acid-free paper

9 8 7 6 5 4 3 2 1

springer.com

This book is dedicated to Francis and Patricia Villemain

Preface

This volume has its origin in the Francis T. Villemain Memorial lectures at San Jose State University – a lecture series established in 1992 to honor the memory of Dean Francis T. Villemain.[1] All the essays in this volume, with the exception of those by Gert Biesta, Susan Verducci, and Michael Katz, were developed from lectures given as part of the series. The general rubric of the lectures was "democracy, education, and the moral life" – a title reflecting Villemain's lifelong love of the work of John Dewey whose preface to his famous work in 1916, *Democracy and Education*, suggested that the purpose of education was to develop democratic citizens, citizens infused with the spirit of democracy and the capacity to think and act intelligently within democratic settings. Of course, for Dewey, democracy was not to be conceived of as merely a political form of government, but as a shared form of social life, one that was inclusive rather than exclusive and one that was capable of adapting to the changing features of contemporary social and political reality.

Francis T. Villemain's appreciation for the intersections of the values of democracy, education, and the moral life was heightened by his doctoral work at Teachers College, Columbia University in the 1950s – where Dewey's legacy remained a powerful one. But it also continued during his career at Southern Illinois University where he collaborated in compiling and editing the collected works of John Dewey. Villemain was a dedicated member of the Philosophy of Education Society of North America and was the only member to have served as president of three regional societies throughout the country; he also was instrumental in establishing the Yearbook of the Society, formerly known at the *Proceedings of the Philosophy of Education Society*. Virtually all of the contributors to this volume have themselves been leading scholars in the North American Philosophy of Education Society as well as active citizens of that society.

---

[1] Many of the Villemain lectures were published in the journal *Studies in Philosophy and Education*, a journal that Francis founded and edited for many years. The editors would like to express their appreciation to Kluwer Academic Publishers and Springer Science and Business Media for supporting this lecture series and to James Garrison and Gert Biesta, editors of the journal, for assisting in the publication of the lectures.

Although many of the early lectures in the series had core Deweyan themes, the authors of this volume were given a broad range to raise what they thought were the connections among the three concepts in the title of the lecture: democracy, education, and the moral life. They were not confined to examine Dewey's question: What role does or should education play in creating democratic citizens? The latitude given these authors has resulted in a wide range of philosophical perspectives informed by many different philosophical questions. Let me briefly summarize some of the questions raised in the succeeding volume. Some of them are clearly conceptual: How should we conceive of racism, of the right to education, of religious instruction and moral instruction, of the forms of rationality promoted in higher education, of democratic patriotism, of multiculturalism and multicultural history, of democracy and democratization, of inclusion, of the moral emotions of love and hate, of "blogs" and "blogging" as democratic practices, of "identity formation," and moral citizenship? Others are more clearly concerned with making connections between theoretical constructs and established educational or schooling practices. They include the following: (1) How do the practices of modern schooling create different forms of social identity? And what kind of schooling would be most valuable in the struggle against social injustice? How might we promote the ethics of democratic citizenship through a Freirean approach to schooling? (Ron Glass); (2) How might we approach teaching history that develops patriotic sentiments without overlooking fundamental injustice to particular ethno-racial groups? (Callan); (3) How should we think about the role of inclusion in developing democratic citizens? How might democracy function in ways that would make it be more inclusive? How might democracy be relieved of its "colonial" mind-set? (Biesta); (4) How might religious stories function in both religious and nonreligious schools and what can we learn about the connections between religious and moral instruction through the way these stories do, in fact, function? (Feinberg); (5) Within the context of teaching in the university, how might three different kinds of practices – deliberation, negotiation, and social activism – promote the knowledge, skills, and commitments that democratic citizens need to live moral lives? (Robertson); (6) How might the practice of blogging foster the prospects for improved democratic dialogue on issues of social and political significance? How might it constrain and detract from making such dialogue rational? (Burbules); (7) How might different philosophical and moral traditions from Deweyan ones to eastern spiritual ones help students deal with the conflicting moral emotions of love and hatred and even overcome the destructive forces of hatred? (Diller); (8) and finally, what do these chapters, taken as a whole, tell us about educating democratic citizens? (Verducci). Many other substantive questions are raised in the volume, but these are a limited sampling of some of them.

The breadth and depth of these questions illustrate, we hope, how many and varied are the intersections among the themes of democracy, education, and the moral life. The essays in this volume, although philosophical in both their spirit and their intent, were intended for an educated lay audience; they were intended to raise, as well as address, many critical conceptual and substantive questions. In that sense, they aim to foster both serious reflection and additional inquiry into what is truly at stake in the effort to educate in ways that promote moral, democratic citizens.

Acknowledgements

The editors would like to acknowledge many of the people responsible for supporting the Villemain lectures at San Jose State since 1992: Patricia Villemain, Francis T. Villemain's beloved wife, whose unqualified, continuing, and unflinching support and friendship has made the lectures a labor of love for me; The College of Education, particularly Deans Dolores Escobar and Susan Meyers; The College of Humanities and the Arts, especially Dean John Crane (now deceased), and Lavonne Simpson, his administrative secretary; The Office of the Provost, especially Provost Carmen Sigler; Rose Stevenson, Dean Meyers' Secretary – a person who has provided the logistical support for the lectures for the past several years; former Provost Hobert Burns and historian Freeman Butts for their early contributions to the lecture; The Institute for Social Responsibility, Education, and Ethics and especially its recent director, Peter Hadreas; and the philosophy department, especially its chair Rita Manning and the teachers of business ethics, teachers who persuaded their students to attend the lectures.

San Jose State University   Michael S. Katz

Contents

Introduction

Education, Democracy, and the Moral Life: Where Opposites Collide

Susan Verducci

Abstract The chapters in this volume articulate the intersection of education, democracy, and the moral life as a space in which opposites collide. A moral citizen must be able to embody the ability to connect and disconnect, to be patriotic and skeptical, to seek revolution and stability, to negotiate hate with love, and to consolidate and expand one's moral identity. An examination of the constructive nature of the collision of these opposites takes place via the theories delineated in the book and the skills and practices the authors advocate for cultivating moral citizens.

1 Introduction

Off a winding road in the redwood-filled mountains of Santa Cruz, California, lies a quaint tourist attraction. The Mystery Spot is a 150-foot diameter on the side of a mountain where the laws of gravity and physics seem to be suspended. Balls roll up, not down. People stand "upright" at such a dramatic angle that they cannot see their feet. Rain falls to the left and trees curve counterclockwise, the direction they would if they were growing in South America. Skeptics bring carpenter levels and the machinery of science to decipher reasons for these physical anomalies, yet they return to their cars (through the gift shop of course) baffled. Their experience at the Mystery Spot challenges their conception of the laws of the natural world.

The chapters in this book lead to a similar sort of challenge. By the time we are 3 years old, most of us know that to connect and to disconnect are opposite actions. Although we might perform these actions sequentially, both cannot be done at the same time. Patriotism/skepticism, inclusion/exclusion, revolution/stability, love/hatred, and consolidation/expansion are pairs in which each member opposes the other. Or do they? In what follows, I will explore the idea that this book, taken as a whole, points to the nexus of the domains of education, democracy, and the moral life as a place in which Aristotle's law of noncontradiction becomes suspended.

San Jose State University

M.S. Katz et al. (eds.) *Education, Democracy, and the Moral Life*,
© Springer Science + Business Media, B.V. 2009

Where democracy, education, and the moral life intersect, certain opposites collide to become self-contained.[1]

Suspending the law of noncontradiction can be a risky endeavor. Centuries after Aristotle proposed it, the Persian philosopher Avicenna wrote: "Anyone who denies the law of non-contradiction should be beaten and burned until he admits that to be beaten is not the same as not to be beaten, and to be burned is not the same as not to be burned." At risk of being both beaten and burned (and wouldn't one of those have been enough?), below I delineate the theoretical opposites at play in the chapters. I then look at how some of the authors embody the collision of opposites in the skills and practices they advocate for cultivating moral citizens in schools and those that can be learned through democratic citizenship. I do not intend to baffle readers in the way Mystery Spot does; I intend that when they finish reading, they are invigorated by the dynamic possibilities and challenges of a space where opposites collide.

2   Collisions

One of the primary sets of opposites at play in this volume is "connection and disconnection." To connect is to join something/s together, to unite. It is the ability to perceive and understand the relationships between things, people, events, and ideas in the world. Connecting can also be an action, to behave in ways that honor these perceptions and understandings.

A number of chapters focus on how education can and must negotiate a central paradox in democracy – liberty. In a moral and liberal democracy, people must voluntarily and without coercion *come together* politically to be *free*. We must come together to pursue our individual conceptions of the good life. We must connect to be autonomous. These connections must be forged between disparate persons with disparate cultures belonging to disparate groups (religious and secular) holding disparate ideas. For democracy to manifest even in its vastly imperfect forms, connections are necessary.

The chapters in this book also bring to us the idea that disconnection has a forceful and constructive role in our history and current context. To disconnect is to sever connections, to pull apart, to disunite. There are powerful forces of disconnection in the United States, and the world more broadly. First, we have the descriptive fact of pluralism and our normative conception of it in relation to democracy. Although pluralism can be framed in terms of unity and opportunity, the authors in this volume look to the disuniting challenges that cultural pluralism, religious

---

[1] In this essay, I borrow Heraclitus' notion of *coincidentia oppositorum* (opposites collide) and the idea that these opposites can become "self-contained" from Robin Patric Clair's *Organizing Silence: A World of Possibilities*.

pluralism, and pluralism of interests provide. Acts of coming together, acts of connecting for the sake of liberty, equality, and justice, are complicated in this light and yet many chapters in this collection can be seen to articulate the force of disconnection as a constructive one in the intersecting space of democracy, education, and morality. It is a force that, in its collision with connection, can help cultivate moral and democratic citizens.

One particular form of the connection/disconnection duality in these pages is inclusion/exclusion. Ronald Glass, Gert Biesta, and Eammon Callan all highlight the complexity of the fundamental democratic principle of inclusion in their work. Biesta opens his chapter thus: "It could well be argued that inclusion is one of the core values, if not *the* core value of democracy. The 'point' of democracy, after all, is the inclusion of everyone (the whole *demos*) into the ruling (*kratein*) of society." (Chapter 7, p. 101.) He rejects the way inclusion has been explored in the aggregative and deliberative models of democracy because these models (imperialistically) assume that we "already know what democracy is and that inclusion is nothing more than bringing more people into the existing democratic order." (Chapter 7, p. 111) As the only author *not* hailing from the United States, Biesta refreshingly points to the destructive way this conception of inclusion has been applied not only within political democracies, but on the geopolitical level. Biesta then points us to Jacques Rancière's work, in which democracy is conceived of as sporadic, as happening in the moments when the logic of equality *interrupts* the current democratic "police order." The connections to democracy happen through disconnection. Inclusion (connection) transforms the status quo toward equality; it breaks (disconnects) with the "police order" in the name of equality. Democratic inclusion connects *and* disconnects in democracy. Democratization, or the education of citizens, takes place in these moments when opposites collide.

Ron Glass' analysis differs from Biesta's in that it occurs on the level of individual identity formation. It is, however, similar in that the cultivation of democratic citizens challenges the ideological order of society. Glass argues that the process of cultivating democratic citizens in schools is the process of awakening self-understanding of students' connections to historical, social, and cultural contexts in ways that cultivate the obligation to struggle and act toward social justice. This struggle toward social justice moves those on the inside to include those on the outside, *and* those on the outside to work for inclusion on the inside. "[P]ublic schools (as the institution charged with the forming citizens of the state) must build loyalty both *for and against* the state and the institutions of society. Schools must build the capacity for moral and political conflict into the very nature of citizenship." (Chapter 1, p.27) Here, cultivating democratic citizens means facilitating the formation of persons who are both for and against the state and its institutions, people who have the ability to engage in moral and political conflict. Again, citizens in whom opposites collide and become self-contained.

Both Glass and Biesta see democracy happening in the disruption of the status quo. Eammon Callan worries about this; he writes that we cannot simply stop at these disruptions – permanent revolution is inconceivable. We need to also build "durable political structures." (Chapter 4, p. 60) Callan argues that, "[j]ustice and democracy can be no more than moments in a bleak history without them unless they become embedded as at least common aspirations and partial achievements in durable political structures that permit the peaceful conduct of collective self rule" (ibid.). The status quo cannot simply remain shaken and continually in the process of transformation (or revolution). It must be built again (and again, and again) with justice, equality, and liberty as its ideals. Biesta and Glass would agree that some political stability is necessary, but it is in the moments of disruption (or revolution) toward equality that moral citizens connect to democracy. Again, opposites collide, this time in the form of revolution and stability. Moral citizens must be able to contain both.

Callan specifically takes on the topic of the cultivation of democratic patriotism in the teaching of a "genuinely multicultural history." The question Callan poses is how we might cultivate connections to democracy in school (in the form of patriotism) despite the contents of a dispiriting and disengaging history, one characterized by disconnection in the form of inequality and oppression – all of which can result in apathy and skepticism. As Callan points out, a history that recognizes America's inherent multiculturalism is one in which the myth of America regarding free and equal citizenship is debunked; a truly multicultural history shows how we continue to fall woefully short of reaching our values of freedom and equality. He points out that any struggle toward freedom and equality requires that we cultivate patriotism. Without it, future citizens are left disengaged and without a political home. The issue in schools is to balance the need to honour (the disconnections inherent in) our multicultural history with the need to cultivate patriots (connected to the ideals of democracy). Again, opposites collide; to connection and disconnection, revolution and stability we can add patriotism and skepticism.

A second cluster of chapters focuses on different but related challenges in facilitating the development of moral citizens. Lawrence Blum and Ann Diller explore the fundamental human experiences of racism and hatred respectively via analysis of the concepts themselves. Both authors see schools and other less formal venues of education as sites for discussion.

Blum draws our attention to the lack of productive discourse surrounding race. His chapter addresses issues of racial pluralism, and gently alludes to its connection to oppression as well as the role that education can play in creating a civic community across racial difference. Here again, we have the theme of inter-racial community (connection) and racial difference (disconnection) in democracy and schools as sites where common ground can coincide with radical difference.

Ann Diller's work clearly centers on the oppositional emotions of love and hate residing in persons. She poses a way of working with these powerful feelings "keeping in mind our visions of a moral life." (Chapter 9, p. 128) Pivotal in her chapter is the First Nations story of the two wolves. Within each of us are two wolves, a wolf of love and a wolf of hate. The one that dominates our spirit is the one that we feed. Although Diller does not posit constructive consequences of hate, she argues that it is a particular sort of love that heals hatred. If we are to be concerned with delineating and educating this love, then we must start by connecting to our (perhaps unconscious) biases and the hatred that we might be feeding. She suggests that we feed our connections with others "beyond the bounds of any narrow, exclusive solidarity" (Chapter 9, p. 149) and instead focus on reaching out to the "wonders of life" (ibid.,) The love that heals hatred is based on feelings of interconnection/interdependence with the natural world, and the human capacities for loving kindness, compassion, sympathetic joy, and even-mindedness. Diller argues that the educational investigation of these oppositional forces dwelling within us can be critical for the development of moral citizens.

Opposites also collide in Walter Feinberg's Chapter 6 on religious stories. He writes that religious stories have at least three important functions – consolidation, expansion, and constitution. First, some stories function to "bring us together establishing a common standpoint, stamping a shared identity and often a common loyalty." (Chapter 6, p. 89.) Second, some stories function to "expand our identity into a larger, worldlier community" (ibid. p. 90). Consolidating implies a coming together and solidification of moral identity. Expansion implies a spreading out, an unfolding into new areas, a making of moral connections with those outside one's group. Both are at play, perhaps not in the same stories, but within a body of religious stories itself. Likewise, both are at play in the moral citizen.

The theoretical work of these chapters offers a view of the intersection of democracy, education, and the moral life as a space in which the collision of opposites is valuable. This is not to say that these opposites dwell in moral citizens in the same way that they might in opportunistic politicians. They are not held in reserve and served up individually when ambition or some external constituency requires satisfaction; nor are they "played" to position one's self. Instead, the opposites contained in moral citizens are in continual, dynamic and productive conversation with each other. It is their collision that allows for the perception of problems with our particular democratic order. It is their collision that can lead us to configure new relationships in line with moral and democratic principles that we hold. It is their collision that can help us determine and enact courses of action and consider their consequences in complex and nuanced ways. A moral citizen must be able to embody the ability to connect and disconnect, to be patriotic and skeptical, to seek revolution and stability, to negotiate hate with love, and to consolidate and expand moral identity. She or he must embody these opposites in herself or himself.

3   Cultivating Moral Citizenship

A question follows naturally for educators: How might we cultivate the ability to "contain opposites" in future citizens? What sorts of skills and practices are necessary to negotiate a political world characterized by the valued collision of oppositions? In a world in which the law of noncontradiction is suspended, does being a moral citizen entail a sort of schizophrenic existence, one characterized by mutually contradictory and inconsistent impulses, skills, and practices?

Emily Robertson and Michael Katz provide some insight here. Robertson argues that three types of practices are necessary for democratic political life: deliberation, bargaining and negotiation, and social activism. The role of higher education, among other institutions, is to cultivate citizens who are able to engage in these practices. Katz calls for the cultivation of critical literacy, which he defines as the inclination and capacity to think critically and intelligently for oneself and make informed decisions in one's own interests. (Chapter 2, p. 31.) All three of Robertson's practices require an underlying critical literacy; to deliberate, bargain, and negotiate; to be an activist demanding that a citizen be able to identify her or his own position and commitments; as well as to think critically when engaged with others who have different positions and commitments.

Engaging in Robertson's practices requires a "coming together," some sort of connecting, some sort of seeking of, and agreement on, solutions to issues and problems. In deliberation, citizens "seek truth or the best course of action through analysis of the available evidence in a process of discussion with fellow participants." (Chapter 8, p. 117.) In bargaining and negotiating, parties try "to secure their own interests, not necessarily to transcend them through appeal to a common conception of justice or concern for the common good" (ibid. p. 119.). Agreement and political stability are the goals of bargaining and negotiating.

Transformation, however, is the goal of social activism. Here Robertson aligns with Biesta and Glass: "activists work to change the [social] structures they view as unjust" through direct action (p. 121). They are motivated by social justice. Engaging in social action requires engaging with the structures of power for change. Robertson points to the civil rights movement, the feminist movement, ACT UP, and other social movements, as ways that citizens come together to create change. These movements are the instantiations of the sporadic moments of pure democratic disconnection that Biesta and Glass articulate.

Nick Burbules' Chapter 3 on political news and commentary blogging introduces yet another means for educating moral citizens. Not only do blogs democratize choice and access to media information, they also put "the power of printing presses in the hands of millions." (Chapter 3, p. 48.) Blogs can hone some of the practices and skills Robertson and Katz write about; they can contribute to the development of critical literacy and of a citizenry that can deliberate, negotiate, bargain, and is socially active for change.

Blogs also provide another educational avenue for moral citizenship, one that expands thinking about education from formal schooling to lifelong learning. Elsewhere, Biesta (2005) has argued that learning happens "alongside" the actual practices of citizenship. As citizens embedded in situations in which opposites collide, we learn about negotiating their challenges and opportunities. We learn by doing; we learn in the context of being citizens. Political news and commentary blogging can be one way in which this type of citizenship education happens. The cultivation of moral citizens capable of containing opposites cannot (and ought not to) be the sole domain of schools.

Robertson, Katz, and Burbules offer ideas about the skills and practices that moral citizens need that can be cultivated in institutions of education, as well as the ways in which active participation in democracy can cultivate moral citizenship. Still, a question remains: To what extent will they cultivate selves that contain the collision of opposites?

4   Conclusion

This book can be seen to heed John Dewey's (1938) warning that we ought not to end our pursuit of sound educational theory in opposition. "Mankind likes to think in terms of extreme opposites. It is given to formulating its beliefs in terms of *Either-Ors*, between which it recognizes no intermediate possibilities" (p. 17, emphasis in the original). The ideas in this volume do not linger at their poles. Further, the book has not been interested in the intermediate possibilities Dewey mentions – in finding some midpoint in the continuum of connection and disconnection, some midpoint to revolution and stability. In the area where education, democracy, and the moral life intersect, this book folds the poles into each other. The resulting collisions provide us with a different way of looking at the challenges and potential avenues for change in educating moral citizens. The authors' ideas provide us with new problems, new questions, and new ideas to pursue.

One of these ideas is that moral citizens must have an ability to hold in their heads and hearts the irreconcilable. This is not an entirely different proposition from cultivating practices such as critical literacy, deliberation, negotiation, bargaining, and social activism, but it requires further exploration. Moral citizenship requires a particular stance toward oneself, the nation, and the world.[2] It requires a stance that recognizes complexities and oppositional forces at play. It requires a stance that allows one to see clearly *and* to recognize the haze in the same instant. It requires an ability to accept a certain level of cognitive dissonance. It requires an ability to accept the beauty in impossibility and an ability not to become undone or paralyzed by the latter. Such a stance also requires a full tank of the humility Feinberg writes about. The slice of existence in which education, democracy, and the moral life intersect is a space in which the laws of logic are suspended and opposites collide, a space where individual moral citizen-selves contain opposites. In this way, educating moral citizens requires cultivating an ability to recognize and accept the crazy and contradictory wonder of a Mystery Spot.

---

[2] Of primary importance is the understanding that this citizenship is not delimited to our national borders; the intersecting space of democracy, education, and the moral life connects people transnationally. Issues of global citizenship, immigration, and post-9/11 international relationships remain hidden in this volume by a strong focus on the United States. Although inclusion/exclusion, patriotism/apathy, revolution/stability, and love/hate can all be seen as challenges in cosmopolitanism and globalization, this recognition is only alluded to in the chapters within this volume. Unfortunately, the idea of a global moral citizenship remains unarticulated.

References

Avicenna, n.d. Metaphysics, I; commenting on Aristotle, Topics I.11.105a4–5 (Online), November 11, 2008.http://en.wikipedia.org/wiki/Law_of_non-contradiction#_note-1

Biesta, G.J.J. (2005). The learning democracy? Adult learning in the condition of democratic citizenship. *British journal of sociology of education*, 26(5), 693–709.

Clair, R.C. (1998). *Organizing silence: A world of possibilities*. New York: State University of New York Press.

Dewey, J. (1938). *Experience and education*. New York: Collier Books.

Chapter 1
Education and the Ethics of Democratic Citizenship

Ronald David Glass

Abstract In this essay, I situate public education within a vision of its special role in enabling critical citizenship within a participatory, pluralistic democracy. I provide a framework for analyzing the current predominant practices of public education, and assess the degree to which they support individual self-development toward that democratic vision. Finally, I suggest that the ethics of democratic citizenship can guide the reform of public education to enhance its capacity to realize a dream of a democracy committed to justice and the full participation of all its members.

1.1 Education and Democracy: From Mann to Dewey

Horace Mann helped establish public schools in the United States as a ubiquitous part of the communal landscape, and articulated principles that still animate the discourse about schools, even if not always the practice. He voiced a dream of a new society, of a participatory democracy supported by free schools that would mold independent citizens capable of governing their governors. Education would no longer be primarily private and the province of the wealthy, nor focused on training the clerical and community leadership in habits of character and thought suited to superior men who knew best for all. Free public education would no longer be haphazard and merely a form of charity, nor would girls be limited to scant opportunities beyond home-schooled refinement to secure a desirable husband and prepare for the resultant household responsibilities, including training their own children.

Half a century after independence, Mann called for a new institution to meet the new nation's need for new men (and women). His educational vision retained an emphasis on character and morality, but no longer strictly for Christian salvation, but rather for citizenship within a unique and developing social organization,

Ronald David Glass
Education Department, University of California, Santa Cruz,
1156 High Street, Santa Cruz, CA 95064.
rglass@ucsc.edu

M.S. Katz et al. (eds.) *Education, Democracy, and the Moral Life*,
© Springer Science+Business Media, B.V. 2009
9

democracy (Mann, 1891).[1] The Common School promised a universal gateway to all things valuable for rich and poor, girls as well as boys. Extolling Christian virtues supposedly shared by all civilized people, the common curriculum of free public schools could unite a disparate citizenry responsible for democratic community and nation formation. Mann argued that the bulwarks of freedom were intelligence and virtue, so schools should teach the love of truth and reverence for justice, emphasizing impartial knowledge and morality which, unlike material possessions, benefited every member of the community and not strictly the owner. Once acquainted with the past follies and achievements of civilization, citizens could reliably assess society to preserve good and repudiate evil. With similar attention to the enlightened care of the body, temple of the well-formed mind, common-schooled student-citizens would develop their natural endowments, meet their community duties, and face the challenging tasks of democracy.

Mann held that since democracy required the participation of all (men) in governing, this entailed that citizens embody an independence of judgment that made them like mountains that move the wind rather than blowing whichever way along with the wind. But ordinary citizens were unaccustomed to equality and co-responsibility with the most powerful members of society. The Common School universal curriculum insured that nonpartisan reason and conscience would rule the passions of citizens and foster their voluntary commitment to the social duties that could forge the bonds of a moral community and realize the promise of a revolutionary society.

These themes of Christian salvation and morality interwoven with democratic citizenship animated the nineteenth-century movement for common schools (Tyack, 1970; Tyack and Hansot, 1982) but gradually other defining ideological elements acquired priority. With unprecedented industrialization, urbanization, and immigration, schools became shaped into "the one best system" aimed not only at forming moral community members but at integrating workers into the emergent economic, social, racial, and political orders (Tyack, 1974). Just as Mann envisioned schools as the mechanism for forming a new democratic society, later reformers envisioned them as the solution to a wide range of social and cultural problems, hoping that they could facilitate the necessary changes in values, attitudes, and behaviors. The new student-citizen-worker would be properly geared into the modern sources and justifications for legitimate authority, modern work habits and relations, modern time and space orientations, modern family patterns and community relations, modern modes of recreation and pleasure, and even the modern ways of inhabiting his or her

---

[1] Contradictions in Mann's vision and in Common School practices still echo in public education. His supposedly common values reflected a pan-Protestant ethnocentrism, and his curriculum asked various ideological preferences. The school's promise of political empowerment for individuals conflicted with its commitments to the existing social, economic, and political orders. In addition, political expediency engendered limits to access to public schools and their rewards, disproportionately affecting African-Americans (despite Mann's abolitionism), Native Americans, and the poor. Nonetheless, Mann's vision of the special and important role of public education in a democracy remains salient yet today.

own body. Once again, the aims were altruistic, forward-looking, and decidedly liberal even though paternalistic. Certified experts could determine the best form of public schooling, which could then be replicated universally in the firm knowledge that "the best is the best everywhere."

Educators' rhetoric extolled the virtues of a meritocratic system that could meet each individual child's needs in a socially efficient way by utilizing leading technologies. Applying the latest psychology and science in professional, impartial instruction, and evaluation, schools promised equal opportunity for all, and pledged their fairness as a measure of our democracy. Researchers claimed that standardized, sequential curricula fitted by scientific tests to the innate capacities of each student meant that only effort and determination needed to be added to the prescribed studies for success to be within the reach of every boy and girl. John Dewey raised a cautionary voice about this optimism toward the one best system of schooling as the formative engine of democracy, and offered an idealistic alternative vision of his own (Dewey, 1934/1960, 1916/1966). He regarded the new schools as still entrenched in traditional modes of knowledge and authority, and as still mired in confused dualisms. He argued that schools should not be detached from society while preparing students for some future role, but rather they should be living social experiments in democratic practice. Curriculum should not be prepackaged and separate from the interests and needs of students, but instead intimately associated with them through genuine problem-solving activities. Students should come to their studies not through the imposition of extrinsic rewards and punishments, but through the guided exercise of their innate curiosity and intelligence. Moral behavior and disciplined habits were to be formed through the natural force of reflective social activities and their cycle of intentional effort and suffered consequences.

Yet akin to Mann and the other reformers, Dewey had an unabashed faith in the possibilities for public education guided by a humanistic, scientific, nonsectarian moral, and nonpartisan political vision. With responsibility for the formation of the proper and best social life, namely democracy, teaching was a calling with special dignity, one whose moral and political gravity imposed an awesome duty on its practitioners. "In this way, the teacher always is the prophet of the true God and the usherer in of the true kingdom of God" (Dewey, 1897/1964, p. 439). For Dewey, public schools remained the unique institution capable of general social improvement and fostering a democratic form of life among a diverse population (Dewey, 1916/1966, 1980). By providing what "the best and wisest parent wants for his [or her] own child" and "by being true to the full growth of all the individuals who make it up" (Dewey, 1980, p. 5) schools and thus society could become genuine democracies.[2]

Dewey adduced the optimum conditions for achieving this aim, and proposed two criteria that could simultaneously provide the strongest warrant for knowledge.

---

[2] Like Mann, Dewey's unconscious ethnocentrism assumed a consensus on who the best and wisest parent would be, and on what that parent would want for his or her child.

promote democratic social relations, and guide school instructional practices. His two standards became philosophically infamous for not yielding the decisive power claimed for them, yet they reveal a distinct critique of traditional schooling and point to a contrasting direction for organizing education. Dewey asked, "How numerous and varied are the interests which are consciously shared? How full and free is the interplay with other forms of association" (Dewey, 1916/1966, p. 83)? He argued that free, open, critical dialogue among the greatest diversity of groups or points of view possible, in a context of shared commitments that promote the capacity for such dialogue, provides conditions for the possibility of warranted knowledge and participatory democratic life. Such dialogues and forms of association presuppose "a large number of values in common, [so] all the members of the group must have an equable opportunity to receive and to take from others. There must be a large variety of shared undertakings and experiences" (Dewey, 1916/1966, p. 84). Not coincidentally, his criteria evoked the standards for scientific practice and relied on the assumption that logic will decide the outcome of the competition of ideas, values, or forms of behavior. This type of scientific naturalism was Dewey's philosophical common denominator (Dewey, 1957), and he hoped that by following its dictates schools could transcend the one best system model and embody a progressive vision that was more adequate to the demands of democratic citizenship. Schools designed around principles that warranted knowledge and actualized democratic life, with curricula based in projects that integrated subject matter while addressing genuine problems, could achieve such aims. Dewey's laboratory schools promised to form citizens skilled in knowledge testing and production, practiced in democratic social experiences, and committed to the ethical ideals that support the maximal development of every member of the community.

What is perhaps most remarkable about Mann, the one best system reformers, and Dewey is that their dreams for public education were so similar. Comparable hopes continue to animate the public imagination, even as some people withdraw into the narrow confines of privatized charter schools and as politicians seek to discipline teachers and students through the standards movement. Public education remains a unique institution that brings together a wide range of young people in a shared experience of learning and participation. The challenge that persists, now as at the start of Mann's crusade, is to make the public school experience one that realizes a significant measure of its democratic aims so that we can achieve our promise as a nation.

1.2   Education and Democracy: A Freirean Correction

Public schools arguably have been the most egalitarian of all democratic institutions in the United States,[3] though they have fallen short in forging active citizens who help to overcome race, class, gender, and ability injustices. The common

---

[3] Tyack and Hansot (1990) argue this in regard to coeducation and equality for girls and women.

school deficiencies most telling for democracy were largely left intact by the one best system reforms, and Dewey's vision failed to be enacted by many ardent followers (Dewey, 1971) let alone those controlling most of the nation's schools. Schools still embody nineteenth-century ideas guided by industrial and military models of efficiency and discipline, and they successfully integrate workers into the capitalist economic order and form citizens obedient to police and governmental authority. Wittingly or not, schools rank, sort, and merge the masses into an ideological order that unfairly reproduces an unjust status quo. The mechanisms of this ordering process unobtrusively reserve economic, political, and social power within the elite class behind claims of neutrality and equal opportunity based on genuine merit. In recent decades, public schools have come under sustained critique from the political Left and Right. Some Left critics[4] found the curriculum lacking with regard to the history, needs, and interests of workers (Anyon, 1979), racial and ethnic groups (Banks & Banks, 1989/1993), and women (Martin, 1984).

Others identified disempowering features of daily school routines and the hidden curriculum that reproduce class and gender relations (Bowles & Gintis, 1976; MacDonald, 1980). The entire liberal arts curriculum and typical operations of public schools have been deeply questioned (Noddings, 1992), and some suggested the end of schooling (Illich, 1971), but most progressives called for reforms of one sort or another. On the other hand, the political Right condemned public education for failing to serve the needs of business (A Nation at Risk, 1983) and decried reforms responsive to the Left critiques as wasteful and incapable of altering educational and economic outcomes ordained by biological differences (Herrnstein & Murray, 1994). Demanding an intensification of the ordering power of schools through more stringent academic standards and increased testing, conservatives seek the restoration of Christian morality and religious practices in public schools (e.g., Bennett, 1996). Although most Leftist and Rightist critiques largely accept that public schools are uniquely important in the formation of a democratic society, this acceptance has been weakened by a sustained attack launched by the Right that has pressured government to give parents more choice of schools, and to privatize public school funding with vouchers and public schools themselves by charter acquisition.

All these developments highlight the inescapably political and conflicted nature of public education in a democracy, and they accentuate inequities among students and citizens. Educational, social, economic, and political power is unfairly distributed among classes, races, genders, and abilities. Yet no other institution besides public education endeavors even to begin to address these issues. Schools, with all their faults and despite questions about their own causal role in the injustices, remain crucial to a hope for creating more fair and equitable communities. A position synthesizing elements from Mann and Dewey and coupled with a robust politics that handles the conflicts at the core of the debates about schools and democracy

---

[4] I mention examples that helped launch lines of inquiry explored by many subsequent authors.

can be developed through Paulo Freire's theory of education as a practice of freedom (Freire, 1970/1994, 1973, 1994, 1998). To build a democracy, Mann put his faith in the power of reason, the reliability of moral habits, and the universally shared experience of public schooling; Dewey put his faith in organic intelligence exercised through a rational, naturalistic science, emphasizing free and open deliberative and communicative processes. Freire put his faith in the organized struggle of poor people who achieved critical consciousness of the limits faced in their daily lives and committed themselves to action to transform them.

Freire (1984) made the politics of education central to his conception of education, freedom, and democracy, assuming a starting point in a context of oppression, injustice, and inequality. He challenged "banking" modes of education that foster silence, passive acceptance of the status quo, and false understandings of reality (Freire, 1970/1994, 1994). Banking education substitutes memorization of facts for the skills needed to produce and critique knowledge, and substitutes fatalistic convictions for the capacity to make history and culture. It robs people of their own hopes and dreams, replacing them with the intentions of the powerful. Education must enable people to be subjects and not mere objects of history or it risks being dehumanizing. Freire called education that promotes the deepest human capacities "dialogical" to invoke the importance of language in shaping identity and action.

Dialogical education liberates insofar as it is a praxis that combines participatory critical reflection with strategic action aimed at overcoming the constraints that silence the oppressed and prevent them from seeking their own aims. Freire's emphasis on deliberative and communicative action echoes Dewey, and both thinkers build their arguments from the foundation of an ontological understanding of human existence. But Freire extends the relationship of education to democracy into the domain of direct action and struggle against the dominant forces of society that maintain injustice. Freire argued that the deepest human capacities for producing language, knowledge, culture, and history suggest that a participatory, just democracy is the form of life most supportive of each person and community being able to realize their fullest potential. This human becoming and flourishing is embodied in an educational process in which people come to understand themselves as precisely the kind of creatures who have the ability and need to produce culture and history. At the same time, they come to understand that the social structures and practices that prevent this embodiment are oppressive and dehumanizing, and thus need to be resisted and transformed.

Education for democracy must make possible the liberation from the oppressions that deny each person the knowledge and means to shape his or her own future. It develops each person's capacity to exercise the human power to shape the future through his or her involvement in the production of language, knowledge, culture, and history. It entails not a mere understanding or state of consciousness, but a way of being-in-the-world that engages in the real struggles at the core of transforming reality into a just democracy. This way of being, or form of life, questions the raison d'être of situations in a relentless critique of existing states of affairs (Freire and Faundez, 1989), and envisions how situations could be otherwise so that hope can be sustained where despair could easily prevail (Freire, 1994).

Education for democracy (and liberation) involves learning humility in the recognition of the limits and failures of every transformative effort, and learning to be patiently impatient in the face of enormous and unceasing challenges. It prepares people to be "dedicated to the long haul" (Horton, 1990) because the struggles for humanization are an unending duty of existence. Democratic citizenship is a form of life that continuously engages the conflicts engendered by oppression and the denial of some people's most basic humanity.

1.3   Education, Democratic Citizenship, and Identity Formation

While much can be said to critique these ideas (see Glass, 1996), I have here only drawn some lines from Mann, Dewey, and Freire to sketch a vision of education and its special role in enabling critical citizenship within a participatory, pluralistic democracy. This form of citizenship extends far beyond voting in elections, or obedience to the just laws of a nation, or participation in the civic life of the community. I believe it provides a compelling ideal and outlines how public education could meet the profound challenges that confront us in our schools and society as we seek justice and a robust involvement in defining community life. I assume that a nearly just society is a condition for an authentic participatory democracy, and that the struggle for a just society is a key feature of democracy itself and will extend to civil disobedience that challenges the state (see Rawls, 1971). Thus, the conception of democratic citizenship employed here would still apply even if the oppression that now characterizes our society were vastly diminished.

Public schools do not currently support the formation of citizens who have a self-understanding of their cultural and historical power and who are ready to engage in the struggle to create a just, democratic community. But schools exist in broader contexts and cannot possibly bear full responsibility for the self-understandings of their students. Identity formation occurs within the dynamics of bio-psycho-social development and is impacted by a variety of both intimate and impersonal institutions, ranging from the family to religion, the media, and the state. Moreover, these institutions are characterized by contradictory forces, some of which support the attainment of an empowered self and community while others are articulated with systems of oppression that undermine or altogether prevent that attainment. Despite the complexity of the situation of schooling, and the uncertain causal relations between that situation and identity formation, some cautious conclusions can be derived from the analysis developed here.

Some social commentators argue that the postmodern era is marked by increasingly weak ties that have traditionally bound together communities composed of diverse individuals and groups. They suggest that identity formation has become more precarious and tenuous than ever, and that relationships among people are often nearly empty in the midst of widespread personal and social alienation and fragmentation. Insofar as these claims are at least modestly accurate (and ample evidence supports this) students are even more dependent on schools for discovering themselves and for understanding one another. The teaching–learning interactions are moments of possible affirmation at the same time that they are moments of danger in which there is a chance for negation, embarrassment, or further loss of self. A student's sense of self can be perpetually at risk as she or he navigates the identities engendered by interpersonal relations with peers and teachers, by performances on standard curriculum assignments from homework to testing, or by peer judgments of the types of people involved in particular extracurricular activities. "Good" kids get positive feedback from adults and are rewarded with the adults' trust and more freedom of movement within the school grounds and activities. "Bad" kids get negative feedback from adults and are punished by being subject to higher levels of adult suspicion, surveillance, and supervision, and so are given decreased access to school grounds and activities. Paradoxically, being too good with the adults can cost status among peers, just as being too bad with the adults can gain prestige among peers. With their identity always on the line, students know the value of toeing the line and they feel the coercive pressures of the various competing norms of the school environment.

But regardless of the label(s) students acquire (knowingly or not), most recognize that educational success is necessary for economic and social success after school. Students discern that school achievement provides some mobility, whether out of poverty or toward independence from home and adult supervision. They grasp that the form of life in school (e.g., required punctuality, obedience to role authority, passive completion of assigned tasks, accommodation to hierarchical relations, and differentiated extrinsic reward systems) is related to life on the job. Students realize that who they are in school correlates to who they can be in the rest of the world.

With the curriculum and activities structured around an unmerciful series of competitions with guaranteed winners and losers, life in schools is risky indeed. For some students success is beyond reach, and insults to their sense of self will accompany relentless disappointment and failure. Sadly, many of these same students are under similar assault from other quarters of the larger social context. Even the kids who succeed at academic tasks and have a wide range of other social supports feel the need to continually prove themselves. They are pressured to demonstrate repeatedly "that they are good, not bad, that they are worthwhile, that they can achieve, that they have respect, that they are decent, that they can have something of their own, that they can make it, 'get over the system' and that they can be somebody" (Wexler, 1992, p. 76).

Occasions for the affirmation or deprecation of the self are endemic to the ideological framework of the dominant culture, but are intensified in schools when identity formation is at its most vulnerable stages of development. Ideological norms and standards permeate every domain from the most intimate and private to the most open and public, from the most profane to the most sacred. Social identity is imbued with value (or not) in the measure of one's relationship to those standards. One can only be more or less distant from the dominant norms and standards of the day, but never wholly independent of them. Each person's location with regard to race, class, gender, language, and ability norms is a defining feature of his or her identity.[5] This situatedness within ideology affects identity formation and is important for understanding the degree to which schools support the development of critical democratic citizens.

Figure 1.1 represents a person's ontological condition of being situated in a nexus of norms and standards conditioned by the larger historical, social, and cultural contexts. Identity irrevocably embodies historicity (situatedness, or both being shaped by and giving shape to situations) and distanciality (being always more or less distant from the norms and standards). Human beings are born into a historical, social, and cultural context (including their bodies) that sets the possible horizons

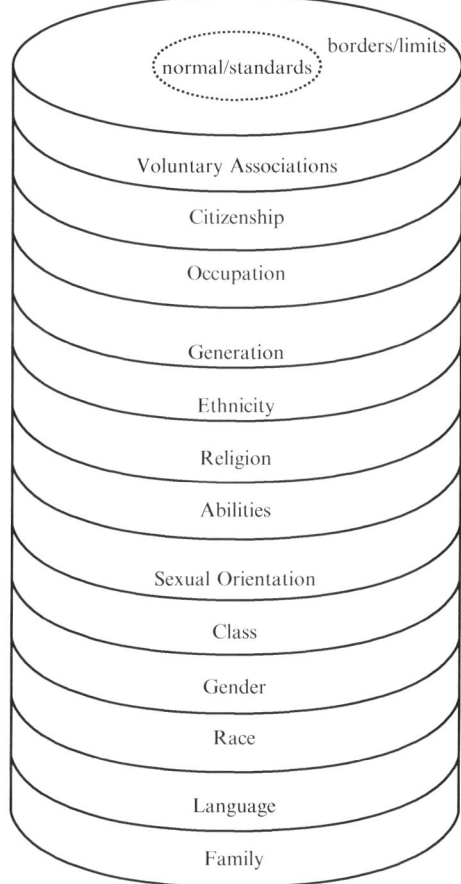

Historical, Social, Cultural Context

---

[5]Other norms also define identity, but these are primary structuring modes for inequities and injustices in our society and schools are deeply implicated in their formation.

of identity. Who one is and who one might become is shaped by the specific customs and rules of the particular family, language, race, gender, class, sexual orientation, abilities, religion, ethnicity, generation, occupation, citizenship, and voluntary associations that constitute one's situation. This larger contextual frame of existence is something that each person is thrown into by virtue of his or her birth and is not something chosen. The norms and standards of family, language, race, gender, class, etc., exert an unrelenting coercive force through a myriad of everyday practices, from the attributions of parents ("Susie is such a good girl!"), to the teasing of peers ("Jimmy's a sissy!"), to the judgments of schools ("You're slow!"), to the actions of government ("Check the box that indicates your race!"). Although shaped and constrained by the situation, we are not wholly determined by it. As human beings, we also make the history that is always at the same time making us. Situations cannot preordain our existence, nor are they completely subject to be made into whatever we individually will. Any particular horizon always contains room to move, and situational limits are dynamic and susceptible to transformation through human action.

While human freedom is ontologically inescapable, at the ontic level of concrete practices, freedom is always precarious. Given that every situation has relentless defining power and limiting horizons, each person must realize his or her freedom through a repeated commitment to one choice or another, to one way of life or another. Each person has to take a stand within and toward the norms, standards, and limits of the situation in which he or she finds himself or herself. The future is open to some measure of intentional, critical reconstruction, and the limits that prevent the realization of a self (i.e., forms of oppression) can be transformed through struggle, through a praxis of critical reflective action with others. Liberation is always a possible dream, realizable to some degree.

The distanciality that characterizes identity indicates each person's irrevocable possibility to choose within the context of the limits, norms, and standards of his or her daily life. No particular identity coincides precisely with the norms and standards. The dynamism of being less or more distant from the customary in each domain of life translates into shifting identity locations over time, for example as we age and mature or as daily activities take place in differing contexts. Thus, each person embodies a unique particularity even as she or he is located within horizons delimited by belonging to groups (ascribed or chosen) and by the background of meaning arising from the social, historical, and cultural context.

The column of Fig. 1.1 represents each person, born into[6] a specific family, language, race, gender, class, sexual orientation, set of abilities, religion, ethnicity, and generation; and who enters into further defining group memberships by virtue of an occupation, citizenship, or voluntary associations. The larger social, historical, and cultural contexts give each domain of existence specific characteristics and horizons; moreover, these contexts are themselves dynamic and in a process of continuous

---

[6] I use "born into" generically since people can be raised outside their biological family or culture or language of origin.

change. All elements in the contexts and within the column (person) are subject to limited intentional transformation. The outer perimeter of the column represents the borders or limits established between each domain and its counterparts, what separates one (family, language, race, gender, class, sexual orientation, etc.) from another. These borders are shifting and somewhat permeable, and perhaps should be portrayed as dashed to reflect a dynamism like the internal perimeter that depicts the dominant norms and standards of each domain. But the solid line indicates the relatively greater strength of these barriers and the force with which the borders are patrolled and policed by group members on either side of the divide. This policing activity to maintain the internal and external norms, standards, and limits takes place in ongoing debates or struggles about just what behaviors, attitudes, beliefs, and so forth are acceptable and conform to the particular dominant expectations. The debates and struggles occur within each domain or group and between domains or groups, and they have interactive aspects as well. Particularly important for the possibility of democratic citizenship and a liberated identity, the debates, and struggles are generally influenced by unequal power relationships.

I will illustrate this abstract discussion with an example from my own life. I am Jewish. Various beliefs and practices set off my religion from others such as Christianity or Islam. Judaism contains within itself a number of primary groupings in the United States, each again distinguished by particular normative beliefs and practices: Orthodox, Conservative, Reform, Reconstructionist, or Renewal. Each denomination enfolds a further plurality of ways to be Jewish characterized by their distance from the established customs. Jews debate the defining tenets of the faith, constantly reshaping the parameters established by the various denominations. Is dancing or drumming an acceptable form of congregational prayer? Must men wear yarmulkes or tallith during prayer? What types of ordained leadership can women achieve? Should women even be permitted to pray with men? What is an appropriate course of study for the Bar Mitzvah? Should there be Bat Mitzvahs?[7]

Some Jews have formal authority for determining the answers to such questions, but every Jew is free to render an opinion and attempt to sway others as to the proper interpretation of the law. When I was elected a trustee of the first Jewish Renewal synagogue in the country, my mother proclaimed that the synagogue "must not really be Jewish" because she viewed me as too far outside the Jewish norms to have such a responsibility. Such comments and dialogues carry a coercive force whose tendency moves people and institutions toward the dominant norms. In some cases, powerful groups establish standards to which others are subject, regardless of their own self-understandings. An example of this at the level of internal border policing within Jewry is a controversial decree by the Orthodox Rabbinate of Israel, the most authoritative judges of Jewish law, that declared null and void any conversions to Judaism not supervised by an ordained Orthodox rabbi. Among a wide range of effects, this effectively terminated official Jewish

---

[7] A Bar Mitzvah celebrates boys' assumption of adult leadership for community prayer (generally at age 13) and a Bat Mitzvah is the equivalent ceremony for girls.

status for many people who regarded themselves as Jewish, and who had been so regarded by both Jews and non-Jews perhaps for several generations. Of course, the notorious example of a similar definition by decree of Jewish group membership occurred at the external border of Judaism when German Nazis passed the Nuremberg blood purity laws. These laws expanded rather than contracted Jewry by effectively making Jews of people with minimal Jewish ancestry but who had never understood themselves, nor been understood by others, to be Jewish. The defining power of the Nazi regime proved itself in the gas chambers and ovens that dispatched all "Jews" equally.

Indicators of similar internal and external border policing can be found in the historical processes of racial formation in the United States (see Omi & Winant, 1986/1994). Consider the meaning of the transitions and contrasting perspectives in identities denoted by terms such as: Negro, Black, Afrikan American, African American, African-American, American of African descent; or Mexican-American, Chicano, Xicano, Latino, Hispanic; or Indian, Native American, American Indian, First Natives, Indigenous Peoples. Importantly, the meaning of identifications shifts with the standpoint and can vary quite dramatically depending on which side of the border the interpreting gaze originates. In addition, these identities have certain defining elements tied to their genesis and continuation in a White dominant culture, despite their rearticulation to empowering perspectives emanating from a group's core. Efforts to subvert the pejorative tags "queer" and "nigger" and to reverse their meaning reveal not only the historical shaping force of labels but also the intensely contested debates within oppressed groups about how to resist the dominant ideology and assert self-determined identities. The location of the borders and the definition of the norms and standards are never within the power of one group alone to determine.

Norms, standards, and borders exercise their coercive power to enforce conformity also in the realm of gender.[8] Virtually from the moment of birth, people are reared to be either boys/men or girls/women. An extremely wide horizon of existence is set in place in light of supposed gender differences that are themselves fixed along other dimensions of identity, such as by religion or social class. People embody distinctively gendered hair and clothing styles, manners of speech and walk, modes of friendship and play, preferred emotions and rationalities, and appropriate roles in courtship, sexual relations, and occupations. In countless interpersonal communications or interactions with the media and other institutions, and in relentless small and large rituals that weave meaning into daily practices, each person is moved (gently or not) toward the dominant norm for his or her supposed gender.

If one enters the gender borderlands, others rush to police the boundaries and return the stray toward the herd. Individuals born with ambiguous or hermaphroditic genitalia suffer policing that can include drastic medical technological

---

[8] Similar analyses as for religion, race, and gender can be developed for the other domains of identity indicated in Fig. 1.1.

interventions to insure a singular male or female classification. Most often in everyday practices, border surveillance and control occurs in barely noticeable micro-interventions that comprise the common sense ordering of the behavior of boys/men and girls/women. Teasing is one such ordinary way to patrol gender and maintain normal behaviors: consider all the derogatory terms boys call one another if they appear to be too feminine, or the labeling of girls who appear to be too masculine. Gay men and lesbians also engage in normative policing actions, and bisexuals can experience pressure not just from heterosexuals but also homosexuals to conform to a unitary identity.

My own family experience provides another illustrative example, though this time of gender policing. My daughter Hannah rowed on a high school crew team, which entailed intensive daily workouts and weightlifting. As her physique developed (she achieved a national top-ten ranking for junior girls) her younger brother exhibited ambivalent feelings. His pride in her strength, which surpassed most boys he or she knew, conflicted with his uncertainty about her muscular femininity. His resolution came in two forms: a tease, calling his sister "Hannah Schwarzenegger," and his own commitment to crew and the development of a physique that reestablished his normative male primacy. This border patrolling took place within a liberated family in the Peoples Republic of Berkeley, in an established counterculture where women were employed in a variety of jobs and men were active caregivers for children. There is no escape from the dominant ideologies that pervade every aspect of daily life, regardless of how vigilant the resistance to them. There are only positions less or more distant from their norms and standards.

Particular persons embody distanciality within specific, dynamic historical and cultural developments, within horizons delimited by norms and standards whose coercive force ebbs and flows. Given the great diversity of ways to inhabit any identity, there is not a singular mode of being Black, Native American, Chicano, White, Jewish, Catholic, male, female, rich, poor, an English speaker, smart, able, a son or daughter, and so on. The debates and struggles to normalize one way of being or another occur within inequitable and unjust contexts sometimes skewed by severe power imbalances. Identity choices do not get made in an equal opportunity environment. The dominant ideologies of race, class, gender, and abilities deeply impact identity formation and access to social, economic, and political power and privileges. They favor certain identities and facilitate self-realization for those who match the normative standards. Who one "is" (and who one is permitted to be) has material consequences for individuals and the broader culture. Some choices require greater sacrifices and must overcome greater challenges. But in any case the process of identity formation is a historical, social, and cultural necessity that embodies the freedom that makes people human beings and more than machines or brutes. To be denied the capacity to achieve one's own self is to be dehumanized.

This analysis of historicity and distanciality clears the way to assess school practices in relation to the degree to which they enable students to achieve a self-understanding that brings these features of human existence into play. Without a grasp of the cultural and historical formation of their identities within unequal and unjust power relationships, students cannot fully know who they are and who they might become. In addition, this ignorance hinders their capacity to engage success-fully in the struggle to create a just democratic community. Self-determination is essential for democratic life, and public schools are charged with building a citi-zenry up to the rigors and challenges thus entailed. But schools now differentially enable self-realization and full citizenship, supporting some and not others in freely expressing the deep human need to make history and culture. If public schools are to take responsibility for fostering the possibility of a participatory democracy, they must reorder the aims that animate and structure their activities, from the content of the curriculum to the form of human relationships fostered. The following sec-tion outlines a framework that measures public schools on these dimensions and points toward reforms that can develop more critical, active citizens and thus per-haps lead to a more just democracy.

1.4   Anybody, Nobody, and Somebody in School

Insofar as schools create identities that conform to the dominant norms and stand-ards, they are making an Anybody of everybody. Insofar as students do not, or cannot, meet the standards of an Anybody, they are made into a Nobody; or con-versely, insofar as students meet the highest standards expected of Anybody, they are permitted to be a Somebody. But none of these modes of identity are what is needed for democracy. Even the Somebody developed by schools is not (for the most part) the sort of Somebody capable of meeting the challenges of forging a just democratic society. A different kind of Somebody is required, one that embodies the ideals sketched earlier, namely a Somebody-in-Particular.

Ordinarily, we grow up into the ideological orders of our culture with rather minimal explicit instruction concerning the dominant norms and standards. They simply comprise the common sense reality and constitute the background of mean-ings for identity and action. Our competence in navigating the culture includes the ease with which we inhabit and live through the dominant ideologies. Akin to how we acquire (or are acquired by) a language, which occurs through its use in speech with proficient speakers, we acquire (or are acquired by) ideologies. The norms and standards are learned through growing up within them, and generally explicit instruction regarding them only occurs when they break down or fail to operate smoothly. When the dominant ideology functions smoothly, one acts and believes more or less like Anyone else.

To illustrate this, consider the trivial acquisition of the rules for elevator riding by way of ordinary unreflective experiences in industrialized countries. Simply by riding in enough elevators, and without any explicit instruction, we learn the rules. We know that we summon the elevator by pushing the desired up or down button near the doors, enter the elevator when the doors open, push the button for our des-tination floor, move to the rear of the elevator, turn to face the doors, focus our gaze on the lighted floor indicators, cease conversation or lower our voices, exchange no more than pleasantries with unknown persons, and so on. If a rider fails to obey the order for elevator riding, the other passengers feel uncomfortable, sensing danger or that something is wrong with the nonconforming rider. In my youth, I rode elevators at a major research university medical center with a friend of mine doing a handstand, both of us appropriately attired in long white medical lab coats and carrying on a normal conversation. When the doors opened people often declined even to enter the elevator. Ideology rule breaking is disconcerting to say the least! Just as we grow up into an elevator-riding order, we grow up into language, race, gender, class, and ability orders. People develop a second nature sense for what is right and proper, appropriate and expected, in a countless array of situations. The ability to rapidly read situations and sense how to conform to its norms and standards enables people to function like a native in the cultures in which they are at home. In foreign settings people may feel ill at ease, and as strangers to the customs they have to work hard to read the cues that indicate what is expected of them.

Schools are among the primary institutions that construct the common sense of our culture, establishing in everybody's habits of thought, feeling, and action the norms, standards, and rules that guide how Anyone is to be. The explicit and implicit curricula facilitate normative "elevator riding" and the embodiment of the dominant culture. Through the normal operation of their everyday practices, schools reveal the nature of the language, race, class, gender, and ability orders, and make clear to students just how to fit into those orders and what is expected based on their location within them. Students are expected to conform to fixed schedules of attendance and paces of learning, and then they are ranked and sorted according to their capacity and willingness to speak and write correctly, to display appropriate deference to teachers and administrators (regardless of their demonstrated qualities of character or knowledge), and to accept without complaint the standardized assessment of their learning.

Anybody in school learns to blame only herself or himself if she or he does not meet the school's expectations, and she or he is led to accept the validity of school academic performances as the measure of her or his social, economic, and political worth and opportunities beyond school. Anybody in school learns that the advanced academic tracks are not primarily for students of color,[9] and that math and science courses are not primarily for girls. Anybody in school knows that academically oriented extracurricular activities are more likely to have a majority of White students involved and in leadership positions, and that certain sports like football and basketball are more likely to have a majority of students of color on the rosters. Anybody in school understands that racial and ethnic groups largely keep to themselves during lunch periods, and that these lines are also generally not crossed for dating or other social activities. Anybody in school realizes that reading and writing in Standard English are the primary rewarded skills, and that musical or artistic

---

[9]Fordham (1996) studies racial identity and its relationship to academic success. By acceding to the notion that academic success is an attribute of being White, African-American students foster a form of resistance identity that reinscribes the racist ideology that attributes higher intelligence and academic abilities to Whites.

talent may be nice for entertainment purposes or padding a college application but little else. These are some of the ways that Anybody is in a real school.[10]

Anybody in school knows that a student who does not wear the right clothes, talk the right talk, walk the right walk, live in the right neighborhood, take the right classes, get the right grades, pass muster with the right teachers, or who is not part of the right clique, is just a Nobody. A Nobody is not expected to contribute much to the school or community, to have any intelligence, or know much of value, to be articulate or say much that Anybody wants to hear. A Nobody is likely to be bad and to come from a bad family, likely to be dangerous and violent, likely to be sexually promiscuous, and likely not to take school seriously. A Nobody can only look to his or her own moral shortcomings as the cause of the surveillance and punishment that are allotted to him or her in school and in life. A Nobody's failure is his or her own doing because every Nobody had the same opportunity as Anybody to be successful and become Somebody.

To be Somebody in school means being among the best of Anybody. A Somebody is recognized by adults as exemplary for every Anybody and Nobody. Anybody in school knows a Somebody gets the highest grades, excels in the activities that bring prestige to the school from the community, or is exceptionally good. Anybody knows that a Somebody, unlike a Nobody, gets special favored treatment by the teachers and administrators. Anybody knows that a Somebody has the best ideas, makes the best leader, contributes the most to the school, and deserves special privileges. A Somebody gets invited to the hottest parties, gets elected to student government, gets the favored summer jobs, and gets to go to the elite colleges. Not just Anybody can be a Somebody in school, only those who earn and deserve it.

But even a Somebody in school may not be the sort of citizen needed for a just democracy if they are only a Somebody-like-an-Anybody. A Somebody-like-an-Anybody does not challenge the dominant norms and standards, does not question authority, and does not work against the school order that reinscribes the unjust social order. This kind of Somebody is just as uncritical and submerged in the dominant ideology as is the Somebody-like-a-Nobody. A Somebody-like-a-Nobody stakes his or her identity on being just as bad as the Somebody-like-an-Anybody is good. In contrast to the Somebody-like-an-Anybody who achieves an identity through conformity to the schools' expectations, a Somebody-like-a-Nobody is the baddest of the bad who makes it big by turning marginality into a virtue. The identities of these sorts of Somebody leave intact the inequities and injustices of the status quo whose very standards are the basis of who they are.[11] These Somebodies are unlikely to fulfill their own potential let alone create the conditions for the

---

[10] Tyack and Cuban (1995) discuss the historical force of the "grammar of schooling" in defining how a "real school" is ordered and examine how these norms and expectations resist reforms intended to serve the needs of students disadvantaged by the current arrangements.

[11] Willis (1981) showed that working class boys' resistance to certain school norms still perpetuated certain other norms, particularly racist and sexist ones, and proved futile in changing the oppressive conditions of their lives.

self-determination of their Anybody and Nobody peers. Only rarely will these Somebodies understand the dynamics of identity formation or grasp the ineliminable human power to make history and culture in order to diminish the coercive force of the dominant ideologies. The Somebodies created by schools are no more able than the Nobodies and Anybodies to become the kind of critical citizen needed if we are to struggle together to form a just democracy.

A Somebody who understands the process of identity formation within historical, social, and cultural horizons, and who is committed to his or her own freedom and responsibility in that context, is a Somebody-in-Particular. A Somebody-in-Particular grasps that human historicity and distanciality entail that everybody is shaped to some degree by the dominant norms and standards of the day which are always being defined through struggles and debates which Anybody and Nobody can enter into. A Somebody-in-Particular recognizes that insofar as everybody is such a Somebody, then the ideological order of society is at risk. A Somebody-in-Particular respects differences and builds groups in which differences constitute strengths. A Somebody-in-Particular works toward collective actions that transform the limits of situations preventing everybody from becoming a Somebody-in-Particular.

Schools have good ontological reasons for facilitating students' critical consciousness of identity formation and enabling everybody to become a Somebody-in-Particular because only such people can achieve the deepest human possibilities for themselves. The curriculum would need to investigate ideology so that norms that support inequities and injustice can be questioned and transformed through direct action. Schools committed to the development of a critical participatory democracy refuse to make Nobodies of Anybody. Instead, they recognize that everybody's voice needs to be heard and honored. Democratic schools value and respect everybody. Everybody produces knowledge and culture and has something important to contribute. Everybody needs to love and be loved, and needs to belong to a community that promotes everybody's maximum potential development. Only by enabling everybody to be the unique Somebody-in-Particular she or he wants and needs to be can schools foster the formation of citizens who will have an enduring commitment to creating just democratic communities.

1.5   Education and the Ethics of Democratic Citizenship

The previous section argued from an ontological point of view that schools should foster identity formation supporting everyone to become a Somebody-in-Particular, and this section provides a moral and political argument that justifies a similar conclusion. Dewey and Freire claimed that the conditions that create the possibility to shape an identity for oneself and to create history and culture are intimately related to the conditions that create the possibility of a just democratic society.

The ideal of a person sketched earlier from their theories focused on procedural and relational matters and noted the importance of respectful dialogue among equals, open communication, critical analysis of both self and situation, and action directed at transforming limits or barriers to the achievement of a self. These conditions are crucial to the embodiment of freedom and the creation of history and culture, and so are foundational to a fully realized human existence. Yet it is important to recognize that this ideal can be made concrete in many different ways, and that other ideals of the person may be similarly compelling and conducive to the formation of democratic life.

Hampshire (1983) has argued that morality is akin to natural languages, and the diversity found in both languages and moral outlooks should be considered primordial. These kinds of diversity in fact establish central aspects of the identity of particular groups that become referential touchstones within the group and among groups. What is most challenging for a democratic way of life in a pluralistic society with a recognized diversity of moral ideals is that "the presupposition that there is a natural and normal harmony between conflicting moral requirements becomes questionable" (Hampshire, 1983, p. 142). Both moral diversity and conflicts between different moral systems must then be taken as a given of social life.

There is no moral arbiter outside the competing forms of life each with particular moral ideals and conceptions of the good life, nor can there be an appeal to human nature to yield a decisive resolution of the disagreements. Given that forms of life are ideologically infused and structured around conventional norms and standards into which one simply grows up, an analytic regression to an authentic, primal self beneath the normatively shaped one is impossible. Just as natural languages achieve their specificity within discourses shaped by regimes of truth and constraining power relationships that establish certain preferred modes of speaking and meaning (Foucault, 1972, 1973), so moral formation occurs within weighted and freighted contexts. The standards of the right and the good are constituted by historically evolved resolutions of contested positions, and so each represents only one possible equilibrium among many.

If the diversity of ideals and conflicts among them are endemic to the moral, political, economic, and cultural domains of social life, and if there is no absolute perspective from which to settle appeals, then how can a choice be made among the variety of contrasting claims? How can a pluralistic democracy realistically be expected to function without devolving into anarchy or violence? Hampshire (1983) argued that in such conditions, moral conflicts can only be submitted to a procedure of just dialogue or debate. This thin conception of procedural justice sets out only the minimal conditions required for fair discussion, and would be likely to be agreed to by competing groups even from a perspective only of self-interest. Every group would want a chance for their view to be heard, to get their moral positions on the table for consideration as the right and proper one. The thin conditions of procedural justice as adduced by Hampshire echo those necessary for the dialogue and modes of communication and shared action at the heart of Dewey's and Freire's theories of education and democracy. A deliberative approach to moral life and democratic politics does not guarantee agreement, and it can in fact be socially divisive and permit politically extremist views a broader scope than otherwise (Gutmann & Thompson, 1996).

Even the thin procedural agreements required for deliberation and dialogue have some thickness and import some moral content that may favor some outlooks over others, and some perspectives may not be inclined to tolerate views which appear inimical to the very existence of others. That is, tolerance and respect for differences are deliberative moral values that are anathema to some fanatical views that deny legitimacy to perceived heretical views. Thus even in a well-ordered and nearly just society, conflicts among citizens over what is right, good, and just can be expected to engender significant social tensions and organized challenges advancing to the level of large-scale civil disobedience (Rawls, 1971). The situation becomes yet more fraught with conflict in pluralistic societies where there is neither general agreement on moral, cultural, or political ideals, nor general agreement on fair procedures or trustworthy adjudicating institutions. In addition, citizens who are oppressed by the dominant norms and standards of the institutions and practices of the society have good moral reasons for an attenuated obligation of allegiance to those norms and institutions (Walzer, 1970). Given such considerations and the resultant thin thickness of procedural agreements, it becomes particularly important that democratic citizenship be enacted in multiple realms of daily life, including particularly schools (Gutmann & Thompson, 1996). While the demand for moral community entailed by a participatory deliberative democracy requires substantive commitments and sacrifice of some individual pursuits, the truth is that no other option presents itself other than a power-based social arrangement that defeats the democratic promise.

The obligations of allegiance to democracy may thus entail obligations to struggle for a just society. If citizenship is to mean something in a genuinely pluralistic democratic society, whether it has evolved to a nearly just condition or remains mired in the oppressions of our day, then public schools (as the institution charged with forming the citizens of the state) must build loyalty both for and against the state and the institutions of the society. Schools must build the capacity for moral and political conflict into the very nature of citizenship, into the common ground that supports everybody being a Somebody-in-Particular. In other words, every Somebody-in-Particular not only has good ontological reasons, but good moral and political reasons, for creating the minimal conditions for the possibility of fair dialogue. This means sharing a common obligation to resist the unjust social order and to struggle to transform society into a more just democracy. The obligation to struggle in a way that is fair to all sides, that respects the diversity of moral perspectives and conceptions of the good life, further entails a commitment to nonviolence. Deliberation in conflicted situations and action to transform unjust situations must guarantee all sides the maximum possible safety in their persons and places in order to avert the temptation to resolve disagreements by resorting to the exercise of power or violence. Civil disobedience and nonviolence make moral suasion and respect for all central to the resolution of conflict, and can be understood as a form of public moral education that supports the struggle for a just democracy (Glass, 1996).

These ethical considerations for democratic citizenship are consistent with the needs of human freedom and identity formation. They are suited to a polyvocal discourse giving expression to identities marked by contradictory, multiple, and shifting boundaries, and suited to intensively contested struggles seeking to transform oppressive dominant norms and standards. An education that takes as its guide the ideal developed in this essay is an education that can enable everybody to participate in the achievement of a democratic community. This ideal is worthy of the promise of public schools, and it is not a dream of distant times but is a vision that can be practiced today.

1.6   Concluding Comments

This essay draws on founding visions from educational philosophers committed to democracy and extends these views through corrective analyses. The resulting sketch of an ideal conception of critical participatory citizenship gives guidance to school practices and promise of leading to the formation of a just society. This outline was given added substance by honestly facing some of the most divisive challenges confronting both public education and the larger culture, and deriving minimal conditions for the possibility of moral dialogue and action in an inequitable and unjust context. The forms of communicative and deliberative action that can warrant the political actions required in order to create a just democracy suggest the kind of self-understanding or identity required of citizens who must risk engaging in those struggles. Hope for achieving a genuine democracy comes only with the struggle to build moral deliberative communities always in the process of transforming oppression and realizing the deepest possibilities for human freedom (Freire, 1994).

The elevated tone in the prophetic voices of Horace Mann, John Dewey, and Paulo Freire recognizes the depth and challenge of the calling to teach for democracy. The tasks facing schools and teachers are awesome: awesome in the size of the forces arrayed against every child becoming a Somebody-in-Particular, and awesome in the sacred duty to insure no less an opportunity for everybody. It is far too easy to succumb to pessimism and despair in the face of the savage inequalities (Kozol, 1991) that plague our schools and society, but it is also far easier than most believe to make progress against these limiting conditions. As Nelson Mandela noted in his presidential inaugural address, "Our deepest fear is not that we are inadequate, our deepest fear is that we are powerful beyond measure."[12] Facing this fear means obligating oneself to struggle for a just democracy.

Our human power to create history and culture is perpetually available and we always have some capacity to act to transform our situation. Recognizing our power means accepting our responsibility. Accepting our responsibility means

---

[12] Mandela was quoting Marianne Williamson.

committing ourselves to a practice that seeks little by little, moment by moment, to embody the vision so plainly before us if we want to build our democracy. Our schools and teachers can develop every child's capacities for mutual respect, for disciplined inquiry and truth-seeking, for critical dialogue and fair deliberation. They can develop every child's capacities for compassion and understanding, for responsibility and trust. They can develop every child's capacities for the cooperative nonviolent action necessary to overcome the inequities of our society. Our schools and teachers can build classroom and school communities that promote tolerance and a shared commitment to justice.

While these ideals may seem just that, ideals, they call us toward what we are truly able to do within the sphere of our own existence. If they seem impossible, it seems even more impossible that we would allow ourselves to go along with things as they are. I am ready to follow some other compelling vision if one is offered, but I am not ready to stand still. Democratic citizenship requires of each of us that we get in motion to create today what we hope for tomorrow. Together we have the power of making real the dream of a just democracy.

Acknowledgment   The basis of this essay was my presentation for the Sixth Annual Francis T. Villemain Memorial Lecture on Democracy, Education, and the Moral Life (April 7, 1998) sponsored by San Jose State University. I am indebted to those in attendance for their comments and questions, and especially to Professor Michael Katz, Chair of the Lecture Committee, for his criticisms and suggestions.

References

A Nation at Risk. (1983). National Commission on Excellence in Education, Washington DC.

Anyon, J. (1979). Ideology and U.S. history textbooks. *Harvard Educational Review*, 49(3), 361–386.

Banks, J. & Banks, C. A. (Eds.) (1989/1993). *Multicultural education: Issues and perspectives.* Boston, MA: Allyn & Bacon.

Bennett, W. (1996). *Body count: Moral poverty and how to win America's war against crime and drugs.* New York: Simon & Schuster.

Bowles, S. & Gintis, H. (1976). *Schooling in capitalist America.* New York: Basic Books.

Dewey, J. (1897/1964). My pedagogic creed. In R.G. Archambault (Ed.), *John Dewey on education: Selected writings* (pp. 427–439). New York: Random House.

Dewey, J. (1899/1980). *School and society.* Carbondale, IL: Southern Illinois University Press.

Dewey, J. (1916/1966). *Democracy and education.* New York: Macmillan Free Press.

Dewey, J. (1920/1957). *Reconstruction in philosophy.* Boston, MA: Beacon Press.

Dewey, J. (1934/1960). *A common faith.* New Haven, CT: Yale University Press.

Dewey, J. (1938/1971). *Experience and education.* New York: Macmillan Press.

Fordham, S. (1996). *Blacked out: Dilemmas of race, identity, and success at Capital High.* Chicago, IL: University of Chicago Press.

Foucault, M. (1972). *The archeology of knowledge* and *The Discourse on language* (A.M. Sheridan Smith Trans.). New York: Pantheon Press.

Foucault, M. (1973). *The order of things: An archeology of the human sciences.* New York: Vintage Books.

Freire, P. (1973). *Education for critical consciousness.* New York: Continuum.

Freire, P. (1984). *The politics of education: Culture, power, and liberation*. South Hadley, MA: Bergin & Garvey.

Freire, P. (1970/1994). *Pedagogy of the oppressed* (20th Anniversary Edition). New York: Continuum.

Freire, P. (1994). *Pedagogy of hope: Reliving pedagogy of the oppressed*. New York: Continuum.

Freire, P. (1998). *Pedagogy of freedom: Ethics, democracy and civic courage*. Lanham, MD: Rowman & Littlefield.

Freire, P. & Faundez, A. (1989). *Learning to question: A pedagogy of liberation*. New York: Continuum.

Glass, R.D. (1996). *On Paulo Freire's theory of liberation and education, and nonviolence*. Ph.D. dissertation, Stanford University School of Education, Palo Alto, CA.

Gutmann, A. & Thompson, D. (1996). *Democracy and disagreement*. Cambridge, MA: Belknap Press of Harvard University Press.

Hampshire, S. (1983). *Morality and conflict*. Cambridge, MA: Harvard University Press.

Herrnstein, R. & Murray, C. (1994). *The bell curve: Intelligence and class structure in American life*. New York: Free Press.

Horton, M. (1990). *The long haul*. New York: Doubleday.

Illich, I. (1971). *Deschooling society*. New York: Harper & Row.

Kozol, J. (1991). *Savage inequalities*. New York: Harper Perennial.

Macdonald, M. (1980). Schooling and the reproduction of class and gender relations. In L. Barton, R. Meighan, & S. Walker (Eds.), *Schooling, ideology and the curriculum* (pp. 29–49). Sussex, England: Falmer Press.

Mann, H. (1891). Means and objects of common school education. In M. Mann (Ed.), *Life and works of Horace Mann* (pp. 77–86). Boston, MA: Lee & Shepard.

Martin, J.R. (1984). Bringing women into educational thought. *Educational Theory*, 34(4), 341–353.

Noddings, N. (1992). *The challenge to care in schools*. New York: Teachers College Press.

Omi, M. & Winant, H. (1986/1994). *Racial formation in the United States*. New York: Routledge.

Rawls, J. (1971). *A theory of justice*. Cambridge, MA: Belknap Press of The Harvard University Press.

Tyack, D. (1974). *The one best system: A history of American urban education*. Cambridge, MA: Harvard University Press.

Tyack, D. (1970). Onward Christian soldiers: Religion in the American common school. In P. Nash (Ed.), *History and education* (pp. 212–255). New York, NY: Random House.

Tyack, D. & Cuban, L. (1995). *Tinkering toward utopia: A century of public school reform*. Cambridge, MA: Harvard University Press.

Tyack, D. & Hansot, E. (1982). *Managers of virtue: Public school leadership in America, 1820–1980*. New York, NY: Basic Books.

Tyack, D. & Hansot, E. (1990). *Learning together: A history of coeducation*. New Haven, CT: Yale University Press.

Walzer, M. (1970). *Obligations: Essays on disobedience, war, and citizenship*. Cambridge, MA: Harvard University Press.

Wexler, P. (1992). *Becoming somebody: Toward a social psychology of school*. London, England: Falmer Press.

Willis, P. (1981). *Learning to labor: How working class kids get working class jobs*. New York: Columbia University Press.

Chapter 2
Is There a Right to Education? A Philosophical Analysis Through U.S. Lenses

Michael S. Katz

Abstract This essay is a philosophical analysis of the concept of the "right to an education" – a concept central to several important U.S Supreme Court cases. It provides a rationale and a criticism of two views of education as a right: namely the welfare right to schooling and the right to be prepared for adult life, arguing that neither of these conceptions does justice to the importance of critical thinking in developing educated persons. It draws on the philosophical work of Ronald Dworkin and Joel Feinberg to suggest that the right to education should be viewed as akin to a general moral principle that I call "critical literacy," the inclination and capacity to think critically for oneself and make informed decisions in one's own interests. It also connects its philosophical analysis to the evolution of linguistic usage in the United States, to the history of compulsory education and schooling, and to several Supreme Court cases where notions of education were central to the argumentation. The essay's force is programmatic – inviting philosophers of education to extend the dialogue about society's obligation to provide an adequate education to its youth to contemporary political and legal contexts where this obligation finds its natural home.

2.1 Introduction

In an essay in written in 1982 entitled "Critical Literacy: A Conception of Education as a Moral Right and a Social Ideal," I concluded my analysis of how education might be conceived both as a moral right and a social ideal with the following:

> The ideal of universal education is integrally connected to the kind of democratic ideal in which people can aspire to think and act intelligently for themselves and can continue to develop their own potentialities through creative effort. Such an ideal needs to be reinvigorated and given new substance as a guiding ideal of educational policy, broadly conceived as that which affects educational opportunities, not merely schooling opportunities. To those who would dismiss this invitation to idealism as a fanciful dream, it is useful to remember the lines from Thoreau: "If you have built castles in the air, your work need not be lost; that is where they should be. Now put the foundations under them. (As quoted in Katz, 1982, p. 274)

Michael S. Katz
San Jose State University

M.S. Katz et al. (eds.) *Education, Democracy, and the Moral Life*,
© Springer Science+Business Media, B.V. 2009

> To the degree that the ideal of universal education remains vague, we need to clarify it and give it substance. We need to relate it to the existing realities of the world we live in. To the degree it remains a castle in the air, there is work to be done. The foundations are yet to be laid. (As quoted in Katz, 2004, p. 218)

As I reflect upon the legal, political, and educational condition of American educational policy in 2005 long after two critical U.S. Supreme Court decisions in *Brown v. Board of Education* and *San Antonio School District v. Rodriguez* – both of which invoked the notion of the right to education – these words still ring true. This essay seeks to reexamine the concept of a "right to education" in the United States through the lenses of philosophical and legal analysis. It concludes with the view that Justice Thurgood Marshall's dissent in *Rodriguez* provides us with the grounds for a deeper understanding of how the right to education in a democratic society should be conceived, namely as a fundamental interest – an interest which functions as a general principle rather than a rule-like entitlement to a particular amount of schooling. If this analysis has its intended programmatic force, it will serve as an invitation to philosophers of education to reinvigorate both our inquiry and our conversation about what it means to grant each person the opportunity to be adequately educated for a productive life as a citizen in a democratic society.

Thus, at the outset, we can ask the central questions, underlying both the *Brown* and *Rodriguez* decisions: Is there a right to education? If so, how should such a right be conceived? And on what basis might it be justified? These questions remind us that philosophers of education must aim to connect the normative ideal of developing educated persons to the concrete social, political, and legal contexts of our lives and to the problems we face as citizens living in an increasingly interdependent, multicultural universe.

2.2   Revisiting the Concept of the Right to Education

Is there a right to education? A moral right? A legal right? The answer to that question depends on how we conceive of two things: the notion of a "right" and the notion of "education." The moral language of "rights," elevates certain fundamental interests to a higher level, a more sacred status; usually when one claims "a right" to something, implicitly suggested is that this claim is special and corresponding duties ensue from it. Undergirding our own political ideology is a view that some rights are "natural rights," such as those invoked in the U.S. Declaration of Independence: namely, the right to life, liberty, and the pursuit of happiness. This doctrine of "natural rights" clearly conjures up an underlying metaphysics of "man in a state of nature" prior to his construction of a societal contract; these "natural rights" were viewed as inherent in man's fundamental nature. In some forms of democratic theory, for government to be just, it had to insure that these natural rights were converted into the political rights of all its citizens. Of course, we know from U.S. history that what constituted first-class political citizenry might be highly restricted – with many groups excluded. Thus, when the U.S. Constitution was adopted in 1789 neither women nor African-Americans would possess these political rights of citizenship. In fact, African-Americans, viewed legally as property, would possess virtually no rights. Nor would children possess them. Even white male non-property holders were excluded. Ironically, these supposedly "universal natural rights" were restricted to white, male property holders. And, of course, "education" was not viewed as one of these fundamental human rights.

But moving forward historically, we extended fundamental political rights to non-property holders prior to the Civil War. Following the Civil War, amendments to the Constitution banned slavery and granted, in theory, full citizenship rights to Blacks through the 13th, 14th, and 15th Amendments. Women entered the arena of political citizenship in the early twentieth century. Yet, no universal right to education was being widely claimed by the early twentieth century, although universal compulsory elementary schooling materialized and most states made new immigrants spend some time in school before allowing them to work. Thus, by the 1920s compulsory schooling laws became commonplace and universal schooling became the norm for most industrialized countries. In 1948, the United Nations issued its official Declaration of Human Rights; in it, the right to education was invoked and connected explicitly with the right to schooling. The section reads as follows: "Everyone has the right to education. Education shall be free, at least in the elementary and fundamental stages. Elementary education shall be compulsory" (as quoted in D.D. Raphael, 1967).

Since common sense suggests that attending school is neither necessary nor sufficient for becoming educated, one might inquire why the right to education would be conceived of as the right to schooling. One reason might be that complex societies must insure that their young people are properly initiated into essential skills, understandings, and values critical to their preservation, and schooling is regarded as the most efficient vehicle for achieving that. In this regard, John Dewey recognized that education was a broader process than schooling and that special difficulties accompanied the transition from valuing informal education to emphasizing formal education; thus, he understood that increased significance would have to be placed on schools as the legitimate agencies of formal education. In Dewey's (1916/1966) view, as societies become more and more complex, the more dependent they would be on formal education as the means of cultural transmission.

> Much of what adults do is so remote in space and in meaning that playful imitation is less and less adequate to reproduce its spirit. Ability to share effectively in adult activities thus depends upon a prior training given with this end in view. Intentional agencies—schools— and explicit material—studies—are devised. The task of teaching certain things is delegated to a special group of persons. Without such formal education, it is not possible to transmit the resources and achievements of a complex society. It also opens a way to a kind of experience which would not be accessible to the young, if they were left to pick up their training in informal association with others, since books and the symbols of knowledge are mastered. (p. 8)

What shifted in the early twentieth century was the view that education necessitated widespread schooling. In the nineteenth century and earlier, the term "education" usually meant "training," or "bringing up," as the *Oxford English Dictionary* (1971) indicates. Implicit in the normative concept of education was the assumption that children would be brought up properly (p. 833). Employing this older notion of education, we might plausibly argue that *children had a right to be brought up properly*; they were entitled not to be neglected or abused. The rights of children imposed corresponding moral duties on those responsible for their proper nurturance. Of course, what constituted proper child-rearing was something each culture defined differently. For example, the Puritans of Massachusetts Bay Colony took their moral responsibilities so seriously that they passed compulsory education laws in 1642 and 1648 – laws that spelled out what it meant to be minimally educated, i.e., raised properly as good Puritans. In this regard, all children were expected to learn to read and to understand the principles of Puritanism and the laws of the Commonwealth. No standardized means were required for these outcomes; no minimal amount of schooling was required. However, by passing these laws, the Puritans translated the child's moral entitlement to a proper Puritan education into a specific legal form; in so doing, the parents' moral obligation to educate their children became a legal requirement and the child's right to be educated was officially mandated (Katz, 1976a).

Even in the recent twentieth century, the obligation to insure a child was educated was not always associated with compulsory schooling. In 1972, for example, the old Order Amish obtained an exemption to compulsory schooling beyond the eighth grade on the grounds of religious freedom, persuading the U.S. Supreme Court that their own approach to socializing their adolescents, that is, bringing them up properly to live as Amish adult citizens, was a form of legitimate education. Although the Amish, believing in a strict form of agrarian Christian fundamentalism, offered no formal instruction to their children beyond the eighth grade, the Supreme Court in *Wisconsin v. Yoder* (1971) accepted, rather uncritically in my view, the testimony of Amish witness Professor Donald Erickson that the Amish "system of learning-by-doing" was an "ideal system" of education for preparing Amish children for life as adults in the Amish community. The U.S. Supreme Court cited with approval Erickson's conclusion that the Amish "do a better job in this than most of us do" and the "self-sufficiency of the community is the best evidence … [that] whatever is being done seems to function well" (p. 233).

In his majority opinion, Chief Justice Warren Burger seemed to accept the Amish's notion of education as "the preparation of people for adult life." This criterion for education was the basis for the Amish claim that additional years of compulsory schooling were not necessary. And Burger apparently agreed:

> Respondents' experts testified at trial without challenge, that the value of all education must be assessed in terms of its capacity to prepare the child for life. It is one thing to say that compulsory education for a year or two beyond the eighth grade may be necessary when its goal is the preparation of the child for life in modern society as the majority live, but it is quite another if the goal of education be viewed as the preparation of the child for life in the segregated agrarian community that is the keystone of the Amish faith. (p. 223)

Is this view of education as the right to be prepared for adult life compatible with all societies? Is the cultural life the Amish live within its homogeneous society and its stable adult roles analogous to the cultural life lives outside it? Dissenting Justice William Douglas did not think so. He worried that not all Amish children would remain within their segregated Amish communities; he worried that if the student "is harnessed to the Amish way of life by those in authority over him or if his education is truncated, his entire life may be stunted and deformed" (as quoted in *Wisconsin v. Yoder*, 1971; Katz, 1974). Douglas thought that the Amish children, not their parents, should determine their own educational destiny; he believed they should be treated as an independent third party whose liberty interests were not to be simply identified with that of their parents.

Nevertheless, in light of the Amish decision and the older institutionalized version of education in the pre-twentieth century, we can conclude that the notion of education as the right to be prepared properly to assume the roles and responsibilities of an adult in society remains an intriguing way to view education. What is useful about this view? First, it conforms to a broad, meaningful sense of education as a process more inclusive than formal schooling. Second, it is linked with the idea that parents and the state share responsibilities in aiding youth transition into adulthood. Moreover, it seems to fit well with the various ways societies socialize their youth.

However, let us consider how this of view of education is problematic. For example, does it provide much guidance to policymakers who live in a rapidly changing society? The answer is "not really." On what basis might one consider a person in 2005 "prepared for life" in 2025? 2035? or 2045? My skeptical question does not suggest a meaningful conception of being prepared for life might not be constructed for societies where rapid societal change is a constant feature. In this regard, Dewey's conception provides one stimulating model for considering the challenge of preparing people for a world where change is omnipresent and unalterable. In Dewey's view, education consists in the ongoing transformation of uninformed, routine habits of thinking and acting into informed, enlightened habits of reflective inquiry – habits that are infused with a deep concern for social cooperation and scientific thoroughness (Katz, 1976b). Dewey's commitment to the value of a democratic community was also one that emphasized openness to change and a broad sense of inclusiveness, not exclusivity.

The Deweyan model emphasizes what our first conception of education as a right may not – the capacity and the inclination to think critically for oneself, what I want to call "critical literacy." In a different but parallel view, political philosopher Amy Guttman (1987; Howe, 1997) places her educational emphasis on the political dimensions of "literacy," advocating a "democratic threshold" for all children entitled to the opportunity to be educated. Persons educated to Guttman's "democratic threshold" would acquire the understanding, skills, and character traits enabling them to participate as political equals in the democratic process; they would acquire "a democratic character." This democratic character embodies the following values: non-repression, nondiscrimination, and tolerance as well as the dispositions and skills to employ critical reasoning to resolve fundamental disagreements in nonviolent ways. This is how Guttman characterizes her principles of "non-repression" and "non-discrimination."

> The principle of nonrepression prevents the state, and any group within it, from using edu-
> cation to restrict rational deliberation of competing conceptions of the good life and the
> good society … nondiscrimination extends the logic of nonrepression, since states and
> families can be selectively repressive by excluding entire groups of children from school-
> ing or denying them an education conducive to deliberation among conceptions of the good
> life and the good society. (pp. 44–45)

Dewey's somewhat more communitarian views of educated citizens differ slightly
from Guttman's more classically liberal ones, but both emphasize the power to
think critically. Dewey's minimally educated citizens are first and foremost members of a particular community, defined in part by their relationship to that community; Deweyan citizens do not conceive of "the good life" independently of their
conception of the good community, but I doubt if Dewey would have any difficulty
with Guttman's notion of nondiscrimination.

When we reconsider education as "preparation for life," we can notice how easily this view can diminish the liberating, nonconformist features of critical thinking
for on its conservative, non-liberating side, one finds significant social pressures
towards making children conform to the existing status quo rather than think critically for themselves. Such an emphasis on adapting to the existing social order, if
carried too far, militates again the kind of thoughtful participation in sociopolitical
life that is demanded of citizens in a democracy. P.A. White (1972) years ago
warned us of the dangers of an educational process aimed at conformity:

> We must … guard against children coming to think that anything which is in fact valued in
> any given society ought to be so valued, by developing in them a rational stance toward
> what is highly regarded in their society. This is demanded by the value put on the develop-
> ment of men as rational beings in a democracy and by the commitment to the desirability
> of individual ideals. To support an education for conformity, for conformity's sake, is for a
> democratic society to allow itself to rot from within. (p. 119)

How then do we return to the issue of how the "right to education," came to be seen
and identified, as it was in the U.N. Declaration of Human Rights, with the "right
to schooling?" Despite compelling reasons for distinguishing schooling and education, one notes that several parallel historical shifts – in institutional legitimacy, linguistic usage, and social necessity – worked together to link education with
schooling in the public's mind. First came the twentieth-century shift in what was
perceived as the institutional legitimacy of schooling; prior to the 1900s, in America,
most specialties including medicine, law, and pharmacy did not require specialized
higher education. However, gradually, professionalized higher education became
the only route into these professions. Moreover, as compulsory schooling became
more widespread, the state, in providing mass schooling, would define what counted
as a "socially legitimate education." In fact, since the early 1900s, state-controlled
schooling has been virtually the only avenue for preparing for adult responsibilities.
Increasingly as schooling broadened its social reach and extended its hold over
adolescents for longer and longer periods of time, the older notion of education as
proper child-rearing acquired a secondary significance. Conversely, the notion of
education as "the systematic instruction, schooling, or training given to the young
in preparation for the work of life" (as quoted in *Oxford English Dictionary*, p. 14).
became the dominant view. Ordinary language followed and mirrored the new

social reality. Over the years, ordinary usage has come to reflect the view that education is equivalent to schooling. Thus, it has become altogether common to ask someone "Where did you get your education?" or "How much education have you received?" In these linguistic contexts, "education" simply means "schooling." And none of the powerful critiques of schooling as potentially mis-educative, such as those by Donald Arnstine (1995), Paul Goodman (1962), Edgar Friedenberg (1985) or Ivan Illich (1970), has triumphed over the emerging linguistic linkage between education and schooling – a linkage supported completely, one might add, by the role of educational credentials in our socioeconomic life.

Consider whether two people educated through schooling would have roughly the same opportunities if one were to drop out before achieving his college diploma while the other completes college and earns the diploma. This hypothetical case illustrates clearly, I think, how the state's interest in universal schooling is buttressed by the individual's interest in acquiring the diploma. Individuals' achievements in acquiring the primary educational goods – knowledge, skills, and dispositions – may be intrinsically valuable in their own right but they acquire noneducational value (social and economic value) only through the legitimated recognition of state-sponsored schooling credentials. These secondary educational goods – these symbols of academic achievement – diplomas, credentials, and certificates – have become the surrogates for legitimated educational attainment (Green, 1980); the state-sponsored system of schooling must assume that these symbols of success do, indeed, stand for the achievement of intellectual skills, knowledge, and understanding. The fact that they often do not do so underlies the state's compelling need in the United States today to regulate schools massively to mandate minimal forms of verbal and mathematical literacy.

Thus, the basis for claiming that the right to education is naturally bound up with, or even equivalent to, the right to schooling is twofold: (1) education came to be seen as equivalent to formal schooling; if one is thought to be "educated," one must have completed a reasonable amount of schooling and attained schooling diplomas; and (2) the educational benefits associated with school success embodied in school credentials became critical to the distribution of noneducational goods such as income, employment opportunities, status, and prestige. Thus, not having access to schooling opportunities would prevent people from having the opportunities to earn the credentials necessary to compete in society for the noneducational goods available there.(-) In this regard, the right to schooling becomes the right to those opportunities to earn the educational and economic benefits that result from graduating from school—the diplomas, certificates, and credentials awarded to schooling graduates.

2.2.1 From Brown to Rodriguez: A Shift in the Discourse on Education?

Two important U.S. Supreme Court cases – *Brown* and *Rodriguez* – reveal how legal interpretations of the right to education can provide only limited guidance in the effort to clarify if education should be conceived of as a right and if so, what kind of right it might be. In its 1954 *Brown v. Board of Education* decision, the U.S. Supreme Court tested the long standing *Plessy v. Ferguson* ruling that separate facilities for Blacks and Whites did not violate a person's right to equal protection of the laws. The *Brown* case questions whether legally segregated schools could withstand the scrutiny of this 1896 "separate but equal" doctrine. Although logically, separate facilities for difference races or different groups might be equal or roughly equivalent (e.g., few people object to separate restroom facilities for males and females), in reality, separate educational facilities were drastically unequal. Thus, in this radical, 9/0 decision in 1954, the Court, recognizing the discriminatory implications of segregated schooling, ruled that separate educational facilities were "inherently unequal" and a violation of the 14th Amendment's right to equal protection of the laws. Moreover, in this often-quoted passage, the Court emphasized the central importance of education and schooling in American life – using the language of "rights" to underscore its significance:

> Today, education is perhaps the most important function of state and local. Compulsory school attendance laws and the great expenditures for education both demonstrate our recognition of the importance of education to our democratic society. It is required in the performance of our most basic public responsibilities, even service in the armed forces. It is the very foundation of good citizenship. Today it is a principal instrument in awakening the child to cultural values, in preparing him for later professional training, and in helping him to adjust normally to his environment. In these days, it is doubtful that any child may reasonably be expected to succeed in life if he is denied the opportunity of an education. *Such an opportunity, where the state has undertaken to provide it, is a right which must be made available to all on equal terms.* [Underlining mine] (As quoted in *Brown v. Board of Education*, cited in Yudof, 1971, p. 365)

Interpreters of Brown disagree about whether this paragraph claiming that there is a "right to education" is critical to the legal basis of the case or is mere "dicta." Nevertheless, the language characterizing education as a right is explicit. But what was a right? Was it the opportunity to be educated? The civil right of access to public schools on a nondiscriminatory basis? The answer is not clear.

Now let us move ahead twenty years to the critically important case of *San Antonio School District v. Rodriguez* (1973). In this case, Mexican-American parents of children attending schools in Edgewood Independent School District in San Antonio, Texas charged that the Texas school finance scheme was unconstitutional because significantly less money was spent on their children than was spent on children in other San Antonio school districts; thus, they argued that the Texas financing scheme violated the equal protection clause of the 14th Amendment. One of the central issues in this case was whether education should be viewed as a constitutional right or not; if education was to be considered such a right or even a fundamental interest, the Texas financing scheme would be subjected to strict judicial scrutiny, and a heavy burden of proof would be placed on Texas to show a compelling interesting in maintaining this inequitable financing arrangement.

However, by a single vote, the Court held that "education is not among the rights afforded explicit protection under the federal constitution." "Nor," Justice Powell, writing the majority decision, asserts, "do we find any basis for saying that is implicitly so protected." Although the majority of the Court concluded there was no constitutional right to education, the content of this conclusion is not readily transparent. What was there no constitutional right to? Moreover, what kind of right was being denied? First, the Court did not see itself dealing with a constitutional liberty, such as the right to free speech or the free exercise of religion. Rather, it viewed the "right to education," as a right to schooling. In this regard, Powell asserts:

> Even if it were conceded that some quantifiable quantum of education is a constitutionally protected prerequisite to the meaningful exercise of either right (the right to free speech or the right to vote), we have no indication that the present levels of educational expenditures in Texas provide an education that falls short. (pp. 30–34)

What is critical to the majority opinion here, I think, is its very narrow interpretation of the right to education as a welfare right to a certain amount of schooling. It is understandable that the Court in *Rodriguez* may have feared that making the welfare right to schooling a constitutional one might have opened itself up to having other minimal welfare rights – such as the right to a modicum of subsistence, health care, or shelter – similarly protected by the Constitution.

2.3 The Right to Education as a Moral Principle not a Rule-like Welfare Entitlement

My own view of education as a right differs from that of the majority opinion in *Rodriguez*; it is, however, quite compatible with the spirit of Justice Marshall's dissent in *Rodriguez* (Newman, 2006). What seems required, as Marshall's dissent indicates, is a broader, more flexible notion of education as a fundamental interest, one that rises to the level ascribed for it in Brown, namely that of a right – the substance of which will need to be spelled out more clearly.

So how should this right be conceived? The right to education is clearly not like the right to park one's car in a garage, for parking one's car in a garage is a specific, clear entitlement. On the other hand, the right to education remains vague and necessarily so, since reasonable people can disagree about what it is involved in educating someone – either minimally or adequately. But can we dismiss those fundamental moral interests from being considered as "rights" simply by suggesting they are too vague? No, definitely not. The U.S. Constitution itself enshrines several vague moral interests as legal rights; among them are life, liberty, property, and due process.

So, how shall we think of a "right" that remains reasonably vague or too unclear to define a rule-like entitlement? Here, Joel Feinberg's provocative scheme of rights seems most applicable. Feinberg (1973) characterizes "the right to life" and "the right to liberty" as "ideal directives." Ideal directives, in Feinberg's scheme, are endorsements of more or less vague ideals; by themselves, they do not specify particular entitlements, that is, specific things that one is allowed to do or have. Rather, they function in the same way that guiding principles function; that is, they deserve to be honored and command us to do our very best for the cause that is built into them. Since a degree of vagueness is associated with a principle or an ideal directive, *I am recommending that we view the right to education as a moral principle rather than as a specific moral rule.*

In ordinary language, we often talk about principles and rules almost as if they could be interchangeable notions. However, as Ronald Dworkin (1967) has reminded us in many forceful ways, principles can be usefully distinguished from rules in several subtle but important respects. A rule, according to Dworkin, sets out the conditions for its application and must be applied in an all-or-nothing manner; that is, a rule either applies to a situation or it does not. Rules, therefore, can regulate specific conduct, by permitting or prohibiting such conduct. Principles, on the other hand, are more general than rules; they do not regulate specific conduct **but they do have a dimension of weight which rules lack.** In other words, if two principles were in conflict with each other, one would have to decide how much weight to attach to each principle in light of the specific circumstances. How do principles function in helping people make critical decisions? They function as important considerations to be taken into account in arriving at a decision, but they do not by themselves, in most instances, prescribe the specific decision to be reached.

Thus, my own position is that the right to education is the right to be adequately educated at least up to some threshold, as Guttman advocates; this right does not function as a specific entitlement but as a general principle, an ideal directive, deserving to be honored. As such it has weight and should be taken into consideration in arriving at critical educational policy decisions – not the least of which is the distribution of educational resources to schools or the means used to evaluate how effective schools or curricula are. The principle of the right to be adequately educated leaves the goals and content of education open to debate and to revision; however, I have suggested that one goal is central to being adequately educated – namely having acquired the ability and inclination to think critically for oneself and to make informed reasoned decisions in one's own interests.

Although a full-scale philosophical justification of this principle is beyond the scope of this essay, I will briefly sketch what I think such a justification might look like, and it is one that seems compatible with Justice Marshall's dissenting opinion in *Rodriguez*. It is also a view that harmonizes with Dewey's concern for social democracy and reflective living. People who are adequately educated are equipped with the disposition and the skills to make rational, informed decisions in their own interests. Presumably, considerations of their own interests will acknowledge their relational obligations to friends, family, and members of communities to which they belong, for I do not believe in a view of personhood that disconnects persons from their social relationships. Quite the contrary. Moreover, if the value of "self-respect" is to be maintained within a democratic community, people cannot allow themselves or those associated with them to be treated as objects, exploited for others' purposes, or denied their basic human integrity (Hill, 1973). In this regard, the content of critical literacy involves moral as well as political content.

Being inclined to, and capable of, reaching one's own conclusions and making one's informed choices is clearly bound up with the larger political right of liberty.

Thus, the right to education as moral principle can be viewed as integrally bound up with, and essential to, the broader right to liberty. One may or may not want to view it as a subsidiary right to the right to liberty. I would rather think that the right to liberty loses its substantive richness if the right to education is disassociated from it.

In this regard, one feature of the right to education seldom mentioned, but central to democratic living, is the right not to be indoctrinated, either in school or by one's government. Recent events in the United States indicate the power of governmental officials to distort the truth to persuade people to adopt certain positions they favor. The fact that over 40 per cent of Americans recently polled thought that Saddam Hussein was involved in the attack on the United States on September 11 indicates the ease with which a populace can be misled by official distortions of the truth. And the problem of indoctrination goes to the heart of serious forms of miseducation occurring in universities both on the left as well as the right of the political spectrum.

So, there is a negative right not to be indoctrinated built into the right to education and a more positive welfare right as well – a welfare right to those opportunities necessary for the development of critical literacy. In this regard, then, it seems that the right to education is connected to a broader vision of a democratic social ideal, one in which the individual is entitled to develop the integrity of mind and personhood necessary for living intelligently as a free citizen in a democracy. This broader vision must clearly be connected as well to a system of social justice which does not deprive any child of positive developmental opportunities as a result of race, gender, ethnicity, sexual orientation, or mental or physical disabilities. Nor does it do so as a result of an unfair distribution of social resources.

I suggested earlier that critical literacy may involve both political and moral content; let me expand briefly on that idea. One can clearly think of the ability to think critically in different ways. Let me examine a few of these: First, one way is a form of inductive reasoning, one of whose primary exponents was John Dewey (Katz, 1976b); for John Dewey, thinking critically was bound up with a certain form of inductive reasoning or "problem-solving" involving several steps: (1) experiencing a perceived need, difficulty, or breakdown in ordinary experience; (2) conceiving of a problem to address this need or overcome this difficulty; the problem provided the thinker the starting point for means-end reasoning; (3) formulating tentative hypotheses to solve the problem; (4) selecting what appears to be the best hypothesis; (5) trying the hypothesis out in experience; (6) observing and evaluating the consequences of testing the hypothesis in action. In one form of moral reasoning (act utilitarian), one deliberates about what choice to make in a particular moral situation, identifies various courses of action, and considers the particular consequences that would flow from each choice on the well-being of all those involved. She or he then adds up the positive and negative effects of each choice and chooses the action that creates the best aggregate set of good effects – or the best ratio of good effects over bad ones.

Another way of conceiving critical thinking involves deductive reasoning, involving both formal and informal logic; Socrates often is considered an exemplar of this form of critical reasoning. In deductive reasoning, defective thinking can result from several prominent difficulties; they include: (a) being unclear about the central terms or meaning in one's key claim or belief; (b) using defective reasons to support the belief; (c) making one or more logical errors in one's reasoning; (d) having insufficient evidence to support one's claim; (e) having bizarre or problematic consequences flow naturally from one's position. The ability to construct effective arguments and critique defective ones lies at the heart of this kind of reasoning. In one form of non-consequential moral reasoning, one identifies what may be morally problematic about a particular situation and what moral rights, duties, or moral may be at stake in making a moral choice; one often must balance competing moral principles in light of the particular facts of the case, deciding how much weight to give a particular duty or principle. As Kenneth Strike and Jonas Soltis (1998) point out, the reasoning is often similar to the kind of judicial reasoning in Supreme Court cases; in these cases, judges decide how much weight to give one principle in light of the facts and act in accord with what they regard as the highest principle at stake. Traditional courses in applied ethics aim to cultivate the critical moral literacy of students by initiating them into both consequentialist and non-consequentialist moral reasoning.

Another form of "critical thinking" is what educators have come to call "critical pedagogy" or "critical theory" (Darder et al., 2003). This kind of critical thinking requires more than argumentation but seeing the relationships between intellectual claims and arguments and the way they are attached to substantive political reality – both historical and contemporary. It demands that the critical thinker notice the gaps between the ideal and the real, between rhetoric and reality; it aims to explode false conventional social "myths," even useful ones as "we are all equal before the law" or "we have equality of opportunity in America." "Critical pedagogy" aims to raise consciousness about "social injustice." It clarifies how such social injustice sustains itself, in part, through developing misleading ways of thinking about both the past and the present.

The point here is that "critical literacy" remains a multifaceted, complex capacity involving different forms of reasoning. Moreover, it is undergirded by essential dispositional tendencies: these include: being reasonable, valuing clarity in language, being skeptical about claims made without sufficient evidence or clear argumentation, and seeking depth of understanding about history and politics. The right to education, as I am arguing here, must be viewed as broader than the welfare right to schooling; it requires those opportunities to cultivate the dispositions and skills that underlie a form of "critical literacy." This "critical literacy" remains for democratic citizens to exercise their full-blown political and moral liberty.

Clearly, how would one determine whether one's right to those educational opportunities likely to achieve critical literacy is fulfilled remains centrally problematic; Why? The reason is simply that this principle must function not as a rule but as a general directive or guideline. Moreover, a much fuller philosophical justification of this right seems warranted as well as a richly detailed account of equal educational opportunities. Nevertheless, it seems reasonable to reassert that the capacity and inclination to think critically lies at the heart of what enables a person to experience both personal and political liberty and to live a life governed by such core moral values as fairness, respect for persons, benevolence, and trustworthiness (Dillon, R, 1995). Our own democratic society is committed, in theory, to such an ideal for all its citizens. However, translating this ideal into a lived form of social and political reality remains an ongoing challenge for each new generation.

One should now note that Justice Thurgood Marshall's dissent in *San Antonio School District v. Rodriguez* is not too distant from my position. Marshall pointed out that the status of something being defined explicitly as a constitutionally protected right oversimplifies and misrepresents the issue of its fundamentality. He points out that the Court had previously protected other fundamental interests that were not explicitly or implicitly spelled out in the Constitutions, including the right to procreate and the right to have access to criminal appellate procedures. The fundamentality of education as an interest lies, in Marshall's view, in the "nexus between specific constitutional guarantees and the nonconstitutional interest." If this nexus is a close one, the nonconstitutional interests – in this case, education – becomes fundamental. Marshall acknowledges that "this Court has never deemed the problem of free public education to be required by the Constitution." Nevertheless, his dissent underscores the fundamental interests citizens have in their educational opportunities. According to Marshall, "the fundamental importance of education is amply indicated by the prior decisions of this Court, by the unique status accorded to public education in our society, and by the close relationship between education and some of our most basic constitutional values" (as quoted in *San Antonio v. Rodriguez*, p. 111). Marshall's argument points to the flexibility to be gained in considering "the fundamental interest in education" not as a specific entitlement to a certain amount of schooling but as a principle. Marshall might have enunciated this fundamental interest as a "right," for that is how we often describe and sanctify fundamental interests. But his point was that its fundamentality required strict scrutiny of Texas's financing scheme. Marshall might also have specifically suggested that this right to educational opportunities was a principle much broader than any entitlement to schooling, but his dissent implies that it is. Marshall also does argue quite effectively that our fundamental interest in education is intimately connected to other constitutionally protected values, such as the right to free speech, the right to free association, the right to vote; he might have included the broader the general liberty of participating intelligently in the political processes of our land. Thus, Marshall's dissent seems to function, for me, as a critical starting point for extending the legal possibility that our fundamental interest in education will function as a legal as well as a moral guiding principle.

To conclude, let me summarize the central points of this essay: (1) the concept of "the right to education" is a concept central to our social ideal of providing each person a minimally adequate education in a democracy; it is linked inevitably to our broader democratic vision of universal education; (2) this concept requires philosophical clarification from the standpoint of the notions of "right" and "education";

(3) it is natural to associate the concept of the right to education both with the right to schooling as a welfare entitlement because of the way in which society has restricted the way in which education will be viewed as "legitimate"; (4) that the right to education can also be naturally associated with the notion of "preparing children for adult life" since this notion acknowledges that education is broader than schooling and that parents have traditionally been entrusted with education as a form of proper child-rearing; moreover, the U.S. Supreme Court acknowledged this as a central aim of education in *Wisconsin v. Yoder*; (5) the right to education conceived of either as the right to schooling or the right to be prepared for adult life places far too diminished a value on a central aim of the most minimally adequate education, namely equipping people with the disposition and the ability to think critically and intelligently for themselves; (6) the right to education is more usefully conceived of as a "general directive" or a "guiding moral principle" rather than a rule-like entitlement and that as such it deserves serious consideration in matters of public policy; and (7) that analytic philosophers of education, committed to clarifying the normative value of education, make their discussion of this value relevant to specific historical, legal, and political contexts in education – so that our work is not perceived as irrelevant.

Bibliography

Arnstine, D, (1995). *Democracy and the arts of schooling*. Albany, NY: Suny Press.

Brown v. Board of Education (1954). 347 U.S. 483, 74 S. Ct.686, I. Ed. 873.

Darder, A., Baltodano, M., & Torres, R. (eds.) (2003). *The critical pedagogy reader*. New York: Routledge Falmer.

Dillon, R. (1995), *Dignity, character, and self-respect*. London: Routlege and Kegan Paul.

Dworkin, R. (1967). The model of rules. *University of Chicago Law Review*, 35, 25–27.

Feinberg, J. (1973). *Social philosophy*. Englewood Cliffs, NJ: Prentice Hall.

Friedenberg, E. (1985). *The vanishing adolescent*. Westport, CT: Greenwood Press.

Green, T. with the assistance of Ericson, D, and Seidman, H. (1980). *Predicting the behavior of the educational system*. Syracuse, NY: Syracuse University Press.

Goodman, P. (1962). Compulsory mis-education and the community of scholars. New York: Alfred A. Knopf

Guttman, A. (1987). *Democratic education*. Princeton, NJ: Princeton University Press.

Howe, K. (1997). *Understanding equal educational opportunity: Social justice, democracy and schooling*. New York: Teachers College Press.

Illich, I. (1970). *Deschooling society*. New York: Harper & Row.

Hill. T. (1973). Servility and self-respect. *The Monist*, 57, 87–104.

Katz, M, (1974) The concepts of compulsory education and compulsory schooling. Unpublished dissertation. Stanford, CA: Stanford University.

Katz, M. (1976a). A history of compulsory education laws. Bloomington, IA: Phi Delta Kappa

Katz, M. (1976b). Two views of 'teaching people to think.' *Educational Theory*, 26. 158–164.

Katz, M. (1982). Critical literacy: A conception of Education as a moral right and a social ideal. In R. Everhart (ed.), *The public school monopoly: A critical analysis of education and the states in American society* (pp. 193–223). Cambridge: MA: Ballinger Books.

Newman, A. (2006).Transforming a moral right into a legal right: The case of school finance litigation and the right to education. In Daniel Vokey (ed.), *Philosophy of Education 2006*. Champagne-Urbana, IL: University of Illinois.

Oxford English Dictionary (1971). Compact edition. Oxford: Oxford University Press.

Raphael, D.D. (ed.) (1967). *Political theory and the rights of man.* Bloomington, IA: Indiana University Press.

San Antonio School District v. Rodriguez (1973), 411 U.S. 1, 93 S. Ct. 1278, 36 L. Ed. 2d. 16.

Siegel, H. (1980). Critical thinking as an educational ideal. *Educational Forum*, 45, 7–23.

Strike, K. & Soltis, J. (1998). *The ethics of teaching.* New York: Teachers College Press.

White, P. (1972). Socialization and education. In R.F. Dearden, H. Hirst, and R.S. Peters (eds.), *A critique of current educational aim: Part 1 of education and the development of reason.* London: Routledge and Kegan Paul.

Wisconsin v. Yoder, 406 U.S. 205.

Yudof, M., Kirp, D., Levin, B., & Moran, R. (1971). *Educational policy and the law.* Belmont, CA: Princeton University Press.

Chapter 3
The Democratic and Educational Potential of Political Blogs

Nicholas C. Burbules

Abstract Weblogs ("blogs") have grown up. Once viewed as a personal outlet for daily diaries, chitchat, and rants, blogs have become an important public space that is transforming social and political relations. Blogs are used for many purposes, but political blogs are a locus of community building, organizing, informing, and shaping public opinion. Because they are free for those with access to a computer and the Internet, they have vastly increased the number, range, and diversity of voices gaining an outlet for their views – although with this growth has also come an increase in misinformation and unproductive "noise." Educators are only beginning to explore ways of using blogs in their teaching, as well as ways of teaching students how to use, read, and evaluate blogs for a range of learning purposes. In the political arena, learning with and through blogs creates a number of opportunities for students to express their own ideas and encounter a broad range of challenging views (including, for example, international views) they might have very little access to through other media. Learning to become critical interpreters of news and opinion on blogs, as with other areas of critical media literacy, is increasingly important.

3.1 The Rise of Blogs

More and more people receive their news, information, and political commentary from weblogs ("blogs"), and more and more people are providing news, information, and political commentary by creating their own blogs (O'Brien, 2004). Because blogs are free and easy to create, they have opened up the Web to a rapidly expanding authorship. There are over 70 million blogs today, with more than 120,000 new ones being created every day (Soltan, 2007). Some blogs are individual creations, others are the work of collectives. They are used for a variety of purposes, from personal online journals or diaries, to fan sites about popular performers, to soapboxes for rants on controversial issues. My main interest here are those blogs used to provide political news and commentary (which may include rants).

Nicholas C. Burbules
University of Illinois

M.S. Katz et al. (eds.) *Education, Democracy, and the Moral Life*,
© Springer Science+Business Media, B.V. 2009

47

Blogs are easily updatable: this gives them the character, unlike more static Web pages, of providing a steady stream of new content – indeed, many "bloggers" will admit that, once starting a blog, the desire to post frequently becomes a bit of a compulsion. If you want people to visit and read your blog (and who doesn't?), what attracts readers and keeps them coming back is the prospect of finding something fresh and new with each return visit. Blogs also make it easy to quote and link to the content of other blogs – in fact, some blogs are nothing but content selected and reposted from other sites. This intertextual quality and the common trend of providing a "blogroll" or list of other blogs dealing with related concerns, gives blogs what David Weinberger (2004) calls "an ethos of generosity." Many Web pages, particularly commercial sites, want viewers to visit and stay put (as it is called, giving them "sticky eyeballs"), because the longer you stay at their site the more likely you are to buy something. With blogs, Weinberger notes, their value is to a large extent dependent on providing links and pathways to other sites, sending the reader off to see what others have said. This relational notion of value and credibility stands in sharp contrast to more traditional proprietary conceptions of information ownership.

Finally, another feature of blogs that gives them their particular character is a Comments section: a space that invites readers to respond, post additional points of view, or argue against what was said. This fosters a kind of open space for debate; and while bloggers can moderate, filter, or even block postings in the Comments section of their blog, the relatively freewheeling come-one-and-come-all spirit of blogging tolerates a much wider (and wilder) zone of discussion than can be found through most of the traditional press. To some, this is democracy in its purest, and rawest, form; to others, it is license for irresponsible and uncivil rhetoric. (Indeed, a favorite tactic of those wanting to discredit bloggers is to pick out some ridiculous statement buried in the Comments section and attribute it to the blog's author, as if he or she were responsible for every comment on the site.) There are important larger issues here about competing views of civility in public discourse, where civility is taken as a norm of politeness and reasonable engagement, on the one hand, as opposed to viewing it as a convention of constraint that blocks deeply challenging and "impolite" points of view (Mayo, 2002).

3.2   The Social and Political Impact of Blogs

As A.J. Leibling famously said, "Freedom of the press is limited to those who own one" (quoted in Kline, 2005). Blogging puts the power of the printing press into the hands of millions and millions of people – without editors, without needing advertisers or sponsors (who might sometimes object to what is said), and without the production cycle that packages news or information within a 24-h cycle. Their speed of propagation means that information (and misinformation) can be copied and distributed rapidly, but it also means that errors can be instantly corrected – one need not wait for the next news cycle to issue an update or correction. Blogs are fast, free, and completely unregulated; and as with all things these virtues can be their vices. They are spontaneous, but unaccountable. They express a wide range of views, but they also tolerate superficiality and half-baked, uninformed opinion. They are radically democratic, but they are – radically democratic.

While most of my blog experience, and daily reading and posting, tends from the left end of the political spectrum, all the same can be said about conservative blogs. Some have claimed that since conservative groups often are better funded than progressive groups, the latter have been forced to use the Internet in creative, activist ways because other cost-based media (notably talk radio, or Fox News) are so dominated by conservative voices. But (to be fair and balanced) I would say that all that is good and all that is bad about the blogging universe can be found at each end of the political spectrum, and throughout the spaces in between. The blog world is the Wild West of political news and commentary: watch out for gunfire, and watch out for where the horses have been walking.

This radically democratic and participatory medium has greatly expanded the range of choices – indeed, for many people it has created the very *possibility* of choice – in where they get their news and commentary. This has certain effects too: because I can choose, I can sample a variety of sources, I can judge and compare them myself, I can make my own decisions about where to return for more of the same. At the same time, because I am choosing I do not have to be exposed to views I find disagreeable or challenging to my assumptions, I do not have to be surprised, and while I may be making my own judgments about whom to believe, I may in fact not be well-informed enough to make those judgments wisely. As a result, the political "blogosphere" is typified by insular communities who flock to the sites and sources that reinforce their views and commitments, and ridicule anyone who thinks otherwise.

One can argue what is cause and what is effect here, but this seems to parallel a trend, at least in this country, toward polarizing issues and demonizing political opponents in public discourse more generally. Fewer and fewer public issues, it seems, are amenable to even the possibility of nonpartisan analysis and compromise. And, yes, in case you wonder, there have been sites dedicated to providing balanced, left and right perspectives on issues – such as the "Left2Right" experiment (http:// left2right.typepad.com). But it must be said that their readership was never more than a fraction of that held by bigger blogs at the ends of the spectrum; indeed, that particular site is no longer even active. Perhaps this tells us something.

Blogs are also, for reasons already described, a medium for social networking. The cross-links and blogrolls, the custom of actively promoting like-minded sites, foster multiple interconnections among blogs, and this gives them the character of nascent political communities and organizations. Many blogs have in fact formed meta-blog coalition structures – most notably, on the left, Daily Kos (http://www.dailykos.com), a massive blogging community in which individual blogs or "diaries" participate in, and contribute to, the top-level blog via mediators who read and select from the "best of" what other bloggers within the D-Kos community have been posting. Through this, even obscure bloggers can find their ideas promoted to a much wider readership.

As I will return to in a moment, this medium also promotes a different kind of credibility structure. Blog postings are accountable, not to authoritative processes, but to collective, distributed processes of peer evaluation and promotion – and while these, too, are certainly fallible (the echo-chamber of misinformation can reinforce error just as well as truth), the broadly self-correcting nature of this process of collective evaluation provides another example of decentered, democratic control. This is not necessarily better than more "top-down" sources of evaluation by editors or other authorities; either method will have imperfections and blind spots. But like peer review in other domains, it emphasizes the priority of maintaining integrity across a community of discourse. Moreover, we need not choose entirely between these as either/or alternatives.

3.3 Blogs and the Traditional Media

How are these sorts of blogs being used? First, it is mistake to assume that blogs will "replace" the traditional news media. Blogs are often an important secondary source of news and information, culled from more traditional press sources who still retain institutional advantages in terms of resources, reputation, proximity, and access to political figures and other newsmakers, as well as investigative expertise not available to most ordinary citizens. But the process of selecting and juxtaposing news clips does give the blogger advantages in terms of how a news story gets "framed" – one is not limited to the narrative structure and priorities expressed in the original story. An offhand quote buried in the 12th paragraph of a news article may be, to a blogger, the most important and revealing item in the whole story. Selection, arrangement, resequencing, and juxtaposition can be powerful tools for constructing alternative narrative structures. Does this risk taking things out of context? Yes. Can it distort meaning or even give misleading impressions? Of course. But does it empower blog authors to express novel meanings and different priorities of importance, rather than being bound to the ones enframed by the original media sources? It certainly does.

Besides, all these problems can be seen in the authoritative news media as well. And this is the important point: to recognize that the news is never just a stack of information, but *always* involves selection, interpretation, story-building, and judgment. Blogs are, generally speaking, an alternative means of doing those things: not just providing facts, but analyzing and explaining what they mean. They give people the same tools (including, unfortunately, the tools to distort) that have previously been held only in the hands of a few.

Blogs can also draw attention to a news story by selecting, copying, and disseminating it. It is very common for a blog to highlight an item culled from some news source and ask, "Why isn't this getting more attention?" Others will notice the story via this reference, and copy and post it for others to see. In this collectivized process, the "echo chamber," if you will, bloggers can give a story greater attention and emphasis. Increasingly, this very process feeds back into the mainstream news, which might pay more attention to the story now *because* there is an online "buzz" about it. Political parties and activist groups are learning to manipulate this trend; making controversies into a noteworthy story simply because they can get bloggers talking about it.

Blogs are also, however, an important source of primary news. During the flooding in New Orleans following Hurricane Katrina, there was no better source of pictures and testimony about what was going on for people than that provided by blogs. CNN could provide dramatic helicopter shots; but blogs contained the personal, articulate cries for help. From the beginning of the war in Iraq, readers have been able to follow daily postings, photos, and video from citizens of Baghdad, or from U.S. troops stationed there. In conjunction with sites like YouTube, citizen-journalists are providing a new kind of news – random, raw, and entirely unscripted. Notice, for example, the infamous "Macaca" moment, in which an ill-considered insult, captured on amateur video, which would ordinarily have only been heard by the few dozen people present, drove Republican Senator George Allen out of office – and, with his departure, gave the Democrats a bare one-vote majority and control of the Senate. Think of how the story might have played out in a traditional news account if there had been no video record.

Recollections of the event differ. Some observers recall that Senator Allen uttered the unfamiliar term "Macaca," but did not know what he meant by it. Others believed Senator Allen teasingly called the youth "Mohawk," referring to his haircut. Others heard it differently, insisting that he said "Moroccan," apparently misinterpreting the nationality of the dark-skinned youth holding the video camera. A campaign spokesman for Senator Allen denied that he meant any insult and claimed that the youth was smiling and laughing after he made the joke. Others say the unknown youth ran off in tears before he could be reached for comment.

Blogs provide local, international, anonymous, and nonconventional people the power to contribute their experiences, their stories, and the things they see and hear into the news cycle. In this way, the sudden, the spontaneous, the local, the personal, and the quotidian can be captured and cycled into the mainstream news universe. Notice that CNN, with its new "i-Reporters" segments, is trying to tap into – and normalize – these same news processes. Notice too that political parties and candidates are also learning to create and disseminate what *appears* to be raw, spontaneous video footage for their own purposes – there is no media form that cannot be turned into its own simulacrum.

Traditional news promises credibility, balance, and objectivity as their virtues: they may be slower, but they are more careful and deliberate in reporting what they find. Local, distant, and/or anonymous sources may be providing the facts on the ground, but who are these people? How do I know I can trust them? I will not deal here with the contentious dispute over the mainstream press' degree of credibility, balance, and objectivity – except to say that it is certainly a contested issue. Nor, as with all these matters, is it prudent to romanticize and idealize The Voice of the People either. There are charlatans, fakers, and self-promoting sensationalists in all walks of life. But the most important point here is that one need not choose between traditional sources and more bottom-up reporting; each can be a kind of complement to, and corrective against, the other:

Indeed, readers seem to greatly appreciate the open, honest, partisanship of political advocacy exhibited in many blogs and seem undisturbed by their refusal to pose as "objective." The very concept of "objectivity" itself, after all, is only a recent construct in the media – a twentieth-century response to the consolidation of a more diverse and highly partisan media into single-voice monopolies (Kline, 2005, p. 10).

One of the main functions of bloggers has been as a watchdog and corrective for media bias and error. At one end of the political spectrum, Media Matters (http:// mediamatters.org) offers daily commentary on sloppy, biased, or stupid reporting and commentary. At the other end of the spectrum, people might recall that it was a conservative blogger who first exposed the flaws in the infamous "60 Minutes" story about George Bush's National Guard Service (http://en.wikipedia.org/wiki/ Rathergate).

This has led to a tense, uneasy relation between the press and bloggers. I think of it in terms of phases. Phase One was one of ignorance and neglect: the blog world was buzzing along, but as far as the mainstream press was concerned it did not exist. Individual reporters may have read blogs, but they certainly never referred to them in their reporting. Phase Two was one of bemused superiority: bloggers were discussed, but dismissed as amateurs, sometimes talented and pro-vocative, but generally with very little to say. Phase Three was one of alarm: the barbarians were at the gate, no one could trust them, chaos and cacophony were threatening to drown out the calm and sensible voices of professional reporters and pundits. Phase Four was one of active hostility and scorn, especially as the bloggers started aggressively criticizing mainstream news errors and biases: the term "blogger" became a term of derision, connoting "radical," "extremist," "scandal-monger," and "intemperate hothead." In many contexts, the wild and crazy bloggers have been positioned by news and political figures as a foil against which one's own moderate and responsible claims can be contrasted.

This is not a purely sequential analysis: some of these phases have overlapped and coexisted. Now we seem to be entering a new phase, one of wary coexistence, as reporters do use blogs as sources, just as some bloggers seek the credibility of becom-ing established "brand" authorities, and as more and more newspapers and news magazines are creating their own blogs as a way of tapping into this new audience.

One way to frame this question is not whether blogs will (or can) replace the traditional news media, but rather, what they can do that is difficult for the tradi-tional news media to do. As part of the larger "Web 2.0" phenomenon, blogs can take advantage of a widely distributed collective intelligence. There is power in numbers, and as the volume and variety of available information is exploding, it is only through collectivized processes that it can be sifted through and understood. Somewhere, some people are spending all their waking hours collecting every bit of information about topic X, organizing and interpreting material from a host of other sources, and creating sites that go into more detail about X than any reporter ever could. This might be via a single blog site, or a Wikipedia page, but in what-ever form it draws together collective insights that build upon one another and explore every conceivable facet of the issue. If it is the exploration of a particular conspiracy theory or scandal, no hypothesis or archived document will go unex-plored. Complex issues of policy or legal reasoning will be exhaustively analyzed. Pieces of information from obscure sources will be sought out, as more and more raw documents can be found online, and then integrated with information from other obscure sources. The insights and analyses of some participants will become grist for the mill of others; a collective intelligence comes to bear. These obsessive preoccupations with fact, detail, and analysis (though perhaps we should call them "productive obsessions") require literally thousands of person-hours in investigating, collating, and analyzing diverse information – far beyond what even a diligent reporter could do. Strikingly, this work is typically done for no pay or reward, except the satisfaction of contributing to an enhanced shared understanding of the issue. It is an autodidact's dream.

Credibility issues remain, of course, and it may not even be a bad hypothesis to think that someone with such a powerful preoccupation with investigating a putative conspiracy, or scandal, or obscure point of law or policy might be a little wacky. But in this venue, comments, quotes, links, and collective analyses of one another's conclusions provide what Tom Callister and I (Burbules & Callister, 2000) called a kind of "distributed credibility." In this domain counterexamples and refutations can propagate just as quickly as unfounded speculation or distortion; sooner or later, someone in the network catches up to you – and the reverse side of the ethos of generosity and recognition is a fairly rigorous process of corrective criticism, especially in the domain of political blogs.

When a blogger rises from obscurity and becomes a frequently quoted or linked authority, it is because his or her evidence, analysis, insights, humor, or quality of writing develops a following that finds him or her reliable over time. The blogosphere, both left and right, has fostered some household names with no particular institutional or professional authority, except that they have seized the enthusiasm of thousands of readers: Digby (http://digbysblog.blogspot.com), Glenn Greenwald (http://www.salon.com/opinion/greenwald), Glenn Reynolds (http://www.instapundit.com), John Cole (http://www.balloon-juice.com), Duncan Black (http://atrios.blogspot.com), Marcy Wheeler (http://thenexthurrah.typepad.com), and the mythic Billmon, now retired (http://www.billmon.org) were once unknown, even anonymous or pseudonomynous figures with just a computer and talent. Some had a background in journalism or academia; others were simply citizen pundits who had something to say, and got discovered. These writers, and many others, do not provide just information or just opinion; they provide substantive analysis and insight; they advance the debate in useful ways.

Bloggers don't need to worry about editors or supervisors telling them what they can and cannot say. They don't need to worry about the opinion of colleagues. They don't need to worry about preserving access to those in power, with the attendant temptation to tone down criticism or avoid offense. They don't even need to worry about their audience: while every blogger wants to be read, the prospect of losing readers holds no real threat or danger (unless the blog depends on advertising – see below). The main esteem that matters is the judgment of others in the blogging community, and this is tremendously liberating in allowing bloggers to investigate and say pretty much whatever they want. Except for a few syndicated columnists or media pundits, few people get to develop and express a unique and personal *voice* in how they write or talk about the news. Bloggers have voice, including the voice of outrage. They do not need to moderate or balance what they say, for anyone – and this gives the blogosphere an essential quality that differentiates it from most other spheres of news and commentary.

3.4   The Limitations of Blogs

There is also a danger of over-romanticizing blogs, however. The more people who have a printing press, the more voices there are. But the more voices there are, the more noise there is. The harder it is for a new voice to be discovered. The greater the temptation is to be outrageous and scandalous, just in order to attract attention. The harder it is to shape a truly original point of view on an issue.

From a reader's standpoint, the amazing proliferation of sources is dazzling, but overwhelming: blogrolls and links from some sites may lead you to the ones you really want to find; search engines may help; aggregator and other "meta" sites may find them for you. But it can be difficult even to know where to start in finding these indirect references. And which of these sources do I trust? "Distributed credibility" sounds all well and good, but it only pushes the question back a level. How do I judge the credibility of a blog recommending or endorsing another blog? Why should I expect the number and frequency of links to be a reliable indicator of importance or quality? Would I apply that standard in other areas of judgment? Is the most-watched news network the most dependable, the best advertised, or simply the most skilled at telling people what they want to hear? The reverse side of interlinked blogs is the "echo chamber" effect, already discussed – the process of blogs repeating and reinforcing certain assumptions among an audience who largely shares them, until even the possibility of someone plausibly holding a different set of assumptions can become difficult to fathom. Who wants an audience whose only response is "ditto?"

At the same time, parts of the blogosphere are increasingly taking on the character of the establishment media (Bowers, 2007). Certain sites are becoming professionalized, glossy, indistinguishable from the online versions of conventional news magazines. Talking Points Memo (or as it is being branded, TPM) is a well-established franchise (http://talkingpointsmemo.com). Daily Kos ("Big Orange," its detractors say) is becoming a kind of blog empire. Other individual bloggers, once independent, have been picked up and sponsored by institutionally established news or media sites: Glenn Greenwald ("Unclaimed Territory") went to Salon; Kevin Drum ("CalPundit") went to The Washington Monthly. As I write this, Markos Moulitsas, the antiestablishment founder of Daily Kos, has just agreed to provide regular political commentary for Newsweek magazine.

These establishment blogs also rely heavily on advertising; many bloggers now ply their trade as a living. In 2005, for example, Daily Kos was bringing in $48,000 a month in advertising revenues (Kline, 2005, p. 49). With advertising comes a whole new host of problems (and temptations): By accepting an ad from a person or cause or product, am I endorsing it? Since advertising income is driven by readership, do I do things to inflate my readership numbers – or not do or say things to avoid the risk of alienating and losing readers?

As a small-time and nonprofit blogger myself, I want to avoid any appearance of sour grapes here. These are all fine bloggers, innovators and leaders, who do great work and deserve all the attention they receive. But we have to ask where this is heading: the trend is toward a recentralization of reader choices, as these mega-blogs pull in hundreds of thousands of visits a day, while other bloggers struggle to find an audience beyond a handful. Is this a kind of Web meritocracy at work? Perhaps. But this analysis (often described as the "short head" of high-status bloggers and the "long tail" of all the others: see Bowers, 2007) belies the originary myth of the blogosphere, of amateur citizens finding voice, building an audience, and endlessly multiplying the perspectives available online. In practice, it is harder and harder for any new blog to break into the top tier, and the dominance of a few sites, left and right, largely shapes the terrain for everyone else.

Another aspect of this, as a handful of establishment blogs dominate the stage, is their appeal to political parties and candidates as a venue for their own campaigns. Blog sites now endorse candidates, sponsor fund-raising, organize events, host interviews – and while there is absolutely nothing wrong with this, it is making the establishment blogosphere appear less and less as a kind of counter-establishment grassroots activism, and more and more like the same kind of mutual admiration society that often binds candidates or parties to particular media outlets, and vice versa. Who exactly is promoting whom?

The blogosphere, then, is no longer just the radically decentered and unorganized Wild West I described earlier; it is also a highly centralized and organized domain dominated by a few sites. (By the way, these dominant blogs are typically, and not surprisingly, centered on the two coasts, where other media concentration also is focused.) We now are hearing people praise (or condemn) "the power of the blogs" in political matters. But the blogosphere never set out to acquire political power, except in a vague collective sense; and for reasons I do not need to belabor the prospect of a few blogs (left or right) becoming truly powerful raises concerns that belie the very ethos that drew participants into blogging in the first place.

And so, there is a tension of sorts between, on the one hand, the spirit of radical democratization, the ethos of generosity, and the decentered and decentralized structure of blogs – and the increasing contrary trend, toward professionalization, advertising and brand-building, and the concentration of audience within a relative handful of blogs. Perhaps this is just the sort of Internet Darwinianism one ought to expect; things cannot remain anarchistic and "flat" forever. But for big-time bloggers, the bloom is off the rose. They have entered the domain of Big Business (again).

3.5   Blogs as an Educational Resource

There are many ways in which this discussion is pertinent to education. First, reading blogs can give students access to a very broad range of news and rich, thought-provoking political information and commentary. Teachers may have to do extra work to be sure that this raw and sometimes controversial resource is related to appropriate curricular goals – but because it is free, searchable, and of inexhaustible scope and variety it is too valuable to be ignored.

At the same time, these materials, for reasons already discussed, provide an opportunity to frame educational questions about credibility, how to independently evaluate credibility, and what different kinds of credibility may exist in online venues. Developing a strong critical literacy about Internet content is itself hardly a new issue; but what might be added by the present discussion is to consider the ways in which new technologies and technologically mediated collective processes can help to support and inform these individual judgments.

These reflections on credibility, as well, should change and inform how students view other traditional news and political media: How forms of representation, selection, juxtaposition, and so on, create narratives of meaning that are never neutral. How can blogs and traditional media provide a check on one another? If "objectivity" means anything in this context, it is as a matter of degree, and judging degrees of objectivity – and the many threats to objectivity – can be stimulated by studying how blog sites select and reinterpret material from more putatively "objective" sources.

Another educational goal implied by this discussion is fostering a wider tolerance for disagreement and debate – in fact, seeking out, and not only merely tolerating, conflicting and challenging points of view. There are educational values at stake here, in terms of fostering certain virtues of open-mindedness (in political and in other contexts of belief and value). But there are wider democratic imperatives that also underlie this concern. The political blogosphere has tended to reinforce the human tendency to seek out like-minded perspectives that confirm and strengthen what one already believes. Blogs are not the only place where this is happening, of course. As discussed earlier, the adoption of "niche" marketing strategies by commercial media, the cynical exploitation of "wedge" issues and other discourses of demonization by political consultants, and a growing partisanship and enmity between the political parties themselves have all worked together to create a wider context in which the serious consideration of a political opponent's point of view is no longer either expected nor encouraged. I doubt whether schools will be able to do much to alter these wider trends; but young people, at least, have not been so thoroughly socialized into that polarized milieu.

Finally, schools can experiment with putting the power of blogging into the hands of people, both individually and as collective groups. Class projects can be completed within a blogging framework; school newspaper or journalism projects might take on new forms; teacher blogs may create new ways for them to interact with students, parents, or the wider community about what is going on in school.

Every technology morphs through new uses; and blogs, wikis, and similar "Web 2.0" technologies are already being transformed through the creativity of users, especially young users. Social networking sites like MySpace and Facebook are absorbing many of the traditional functions of blogs. So we are talking about a moving target here. The professionalization and concentration of blogs, from the other side, seems also to be transforming the idea of the radically democratized personal printing press into something quite different. What comes next is impossible to say; but the basic impetus of the Internet has always been to foster new and decentralized forms of information sharing. If blogs get co-opted, something else will replace them. And educators may be in a special position to observe and understand these trends, because they invariably start with young people. But we have to be paying attention first.

References

Bowers, C. (2007). New establishment rising? The end of the flat blogosphere < http://openleft-.com/showDiary.do?diaryId = 13 >

Burbules, N. C., & Callister, T. A. (2000). *Watch IT: The promises and risks of information technologies for education*, Chapter Six. Boulder, CO: Westview Press.

Kline, D. (2005). Toward a more participatory democracy. In D. Kline & D. Burstein (Eds.), *Blog! How the newest media revolution is changing politics, business, and culture*. CDS: New York.

Mayo, C. (2002). The binds that tie: Civility and social difference. *Educational Theory, 52*(2), 169–186.

O'Brien, B. (2004). *Blogging America: Political discourse in a digital nation*. Wilsonville, OR: William James.

Soltan, M. (2007). Tenth anniversary blogoscopy. < http://www.margaretsoltan.com/archives/2007_08_01_archive.html >

Weinberger, D. (2004). The digital future. < http://www.c-span.org/congress/digitalfuture.asp >

Chapter 4
Democratic Patriotism and Multicultural Education[1]

Eammon Callan

Abstract Debate about multicultural education in the USA has been marked by anxieties about the stability of a nation that is both increasingly culturally diverse and increasingly resistant to coercive assimilative practices. A politically and morally persuasive multiculturalism must seek to dispel rather than evade these anxieties. One educational venue in which they must be addressed is history teaching. The possibility of cultivating democratic patriotism in the teaching of a genuinely multicultural American history is discussed.

> Forgetting, I would even go so far as to say historical error, is a crucial factor in the creation of a nation, which is why progress in historical studies often creates a danger for nationality. Indeed, historical insight brings to light deeds of violence which took place at the origin of all political formations. . . . Unity is always effected by means of brutality.
>
> Ernst Renan ([1882] 1992)

> Our memories may now be undermining our ability to progress as a people
>
> Joseph Tilden Rhea (1997)

4.1 Introduction

One of the most troubling questions in contemporary politics is this. How are stable democratic institutions to be sustained in nation-states whose citizens are increasingly culturally diverse and increasingly resistant to the coercive assimilation and subordination that once helped to secure political stability? Americans face this question, along with many other people.

Eammon Callan
Stanford University

[1] An earlier draft of this paper was delivered as the 2001 Francis Villemain lecture in the College of Education at San Jose State University. I am extremely grateful to the faculty in the College of Education, and especially to Michael Katz and Patricia Villemain, for their warm hospitality and stimulating conversation on that occasion. Tom Ehrlich also helped me to avoid some blunders.

To ask the question and to acknowledge its importance is not to suggest that political stability by itself is any virtue. Political institutions can be stable for long stretches of time despite (and sometimes because of) unrelenting oppression. We need not look to colonial Africa or Asia to imagine that possibility. The American Republic did pretty well, so far as stability goes, before its descent into Civil War, and better still in the many years between the defeat of Reconstruction and the partial victories of the Civil Rights Movement. For all but a few decades of the nation's history, Americans have practiced or at least acquiesced in the practice of either slavery or Jim Crow.

The possibility of a regime that is both stable and oppressive might tempt us to say that justice and democracy are the things that truly matter, and if achieving them is politically destabilizing, then so much the worse for stability. The truth in the temptation is that political order must sometimes be disrupted, even shattered, for the sake of higher values. But another truth is as important. Justice and democracy can be no more that moments in a bleak history without them unless they become embedded as at least common aspirations and partial achievements in durable political structures that permit the peaceful conduct of collective self-rule.

The question of political stability (or unity) in the midst of diversity is frequently raised in scholarly as well as popular debate about multicultural education in America. Unfortunately, the question is rarely soberly confronted in what has too often been one of the bloodier battlefronts in the so-called Culture Wars. And inflamed ideological passions are not the only impediment to democratic dialogue. Another is the almost infinite variety of things that can be deplored or praised under the label of "multiculturalism." Any word that can apply equally to corporate advertising strategies, cuisine, and outlandish academic views about the nature of knowledge has to be used with some wariness. (Part of the problem here is the almost amorphous meaning of "culture" in current, including academic usage.)

For the purposes of this argument I can characterize multiculturalism in a rough and inclusive way. As I understand it, to endorse multicultural America is to be well disposed to the nation's growing ethnic diversity and its free mingling of traditions drawn from many parts of the world through commerce, intermarriage, and the respectful sharing of public spaces among different groups. Some markers of group difference within this diversity are *ethno-racial*: they have differentiated groups whose ancestry has long made them targets of discrimination and contempt in America. For multiculturalists, racial oppression is intolerable. And it is intolerable *whether* it is exercised to exclude people from equal status as citizens or to accord equal status on the condition that all must ape the conduct of socially dominant groups in their public and private lives. Ethnic traditions will change. They might take on new meanings according to some (allegedly) purer, more ancient version or they might alter radically to accommodate new social circumstances. Some long-standing collective identities that once had sharply etched boundaries may fade imperceptibly over the course of time or become more internally differentiated than before. There is no wrong in that, and hence nothing a multiculturalists in my sense could have moral reason to condemn, so long as change is not the effect of discrimination and contempt.

I want in this chapter to focus on those ethno-racial groups most closely associated with the demands for recognition and redress for past wrongs: African-Americans, aboriginal Americans, Latinos, and (to a lesser extent) Asian-Americans. This is a disparate selection of groups. Their histories are very different, and so too are their present circumstances and their likely futures. But for my immediate purposes what they have in common is all that matters. The history of each is in substantial part a history of oppression, and though other groups can claim similar histories, these are the ones who reasonably claim that the stigmatized identity ascribed to them endures powerfully in the present. This is no doubt true to varying degrees about these groups, and within each group by virtue of differences in social class, geographical location, and the like. And there is much heated controversy about what "powerfully enduring" stigma really amounts to in contemporary American race relations. But it would take more than a little naïveté, willed ignorance, or outright lying to say that the stigmatization of these groups has disappeared or is merely trivial.

A multicultural America will differ from the America that came before, and to the extent that it differs, it cannot rely on conceptions of civic unity inherited from a nation that defined its unity largely in ethno-racial terms. But if these older conceptions are to be discarded, what if anything will replace them? Will a new civic solidarity that stabilizes political institutions come from new sources? If so, we need a clear picture of what these would be, and how they might be encouraged or at least protected from erosion. If new sources of stability are unnecessary, we need an account of how we could manage without them and still achieve the institutional security in politics that we cannot do without.

An unfortunate aspect of the current American debate about multiculturalism is that all who would reject it have captured the rhetoric of stability and civic unity, which enables many of them to evade or palliate the moral inadequacy of traditional ideas of civic identity to contemporary America. If multiculturalism really did threaten to disunite America beyond repair, then whatever else its advocates could say is unlikely to be interesting to anyone with an interest in real as opposed to Utopian politics. And that is why multicultural nonchalance about threats to unity is so very convenient for those who would like us to ignore other matters of grave moral importance at stake in the debate.

But there is some blame for everyone here. The defenders of multiculturalism have not asked searching questions about stability in the America they wish to bring into being. They prefer instead to talk about the need to celebrate diversity, resist ethnic oppression, and abjure coercive assimilation, as if the importance of these things relieved them of responsibility to address the need for continuous and resilient democratic forms that would permit the orderly pursuit of democratic politics. If we care about a multicultural America, then the education we need must be consistent with a good answer to the question of stability.

I want to explore one facet of the stability problem that multiculturalists must confront. My topic is the teaching of national history in American schools. Only a fool could imagine that the fulcrum of political stability is what teachers tell their students about the history of their country. But the problems of history education are an especially useful way of bringing into focus some urgent questions about the possibility and desirability of patriotism in a multicultural America. By "patriotism" I mean active identification with one's particular nation as a cross-generational political community whose flourishing one prizes and seeks to advance; by "democratic patriotism" I mean patriotism informed by the conviction that the national community with which one identifies cannot thrive save through democratic self-rule.

I shall argue that a multicultural American history is the only morally and intellectually permissible history for its schools. That said, learning such history is inevitably in some tension with the cultivation of democratic patriotism. And democratic patriotism is something we cannot do without if the wrongs that a multicultural history reveals are ever to be righted. To live productively with that tension we need to acknowledge it in our own lives and in our classrooms. And the tension might be more manageable if our students could learn to see their demythologized national history not so much as a source of inspiration – or demoralization, which is the inevitable risk when they expect to be inspired – but as something to be appropriated and carried forward without any glib pride or despair if democratic ideals are to prevail in the nation they will inherit and rule.

4.2 Patriotic and Anti-Patriotic History

Mass schooling in America began in the nineteenth century as a project of nation-building. Public schools would help to create a citizenry primed to ensure the strength of established political (and economic) institutions from one generation to another, and critical to that task was the inculcation of patriotism. Patriotism was defined initially on the basis of Anglo-Saxon religious and racial identity. Schools were dedicated a form of socialization in which ethnic assimilation, the diffusion of a nonsectarian Protestantism, and loyalty to the nation were inextricably tied together. Or at least that was so for those who might be drawn within the circle of "white" America. The Irish seemed very unpromising material at first, but as time passed they gained entry, as did Italians, Poles, and the like.

The traditional patriotic ideal required a supporting national history. The content of the history shifted over time and was fiercely contested in much of its detail. Yet it was contested against the background of largely unchallenged assumptions about the permanent marginality of minorities who could never be deemed "white" (e.g., African-Americans), and the legitimate assignment of others (i.e., women) to a less brutalized form of inferior citizenship which required them to live their lives under the intimate and benevolent authority of their betters.

A set of rules for assigning or denying full citizenship is necessary to the nation-state, but it is primarily the consequence rather than the cause of a shared or dominant sense of national identity. That identity must involve a certain sense of community. Benedict Anderson, a widely influential scholar on nationalism, famously claimed that all nations are "imagined communities" (Anderson, 1991). The ambiguity of "imagined" is important here. In one sense, Anderson is merely suggesting that nations are made possible through the constructive power of imagination. Human beings who will directly encounter only a tiny fraction of the others who share in their common imaginings of nationhood constitute the nation through those very imaginings. Of course, the nation thus "imagined" is not imaginary – a fiction created in defiance of reason. Nevertheless, Anderson is also suggesting that fiction in the form of myth is at the core of nationhood. To identify with the nation as the patriot does is to imagine oneself belonging within a valued community whose past and future bind all together as a people who rightfully claim to rule themselves, and this is not possible, Anderson and other students of nationalism have insisted, without myth.

Schools as engines of nation-building teach a "patriotic history" that inspires and directs the political imagination of citizens in the service of national community. Myth is needed here, the argument goes, because myth inspires in a way that plain facts about predatory warfare, self-serving elites, and downtrodden or resistant masses cannot possibly equal. National myth is so powerful because its widespread acceptance absorbs the loyalties and responsibilities of ordinary citizens within a glorious past of shared achievement, with epic victories and tragic defeats, heroic leaders, and despicable enemies. And the national future in which past glories are reclaimed or current greatness sustained offers a form of ersatz immortality for citizens who keep up the patriotic faith. The grandeur of the great nation infuses the humdrum responsibilities of citizenship, and not merely the sacrifices of war and comparable national crises, with a meaning they could not otherwise have. Nevertheless, if the nation as myth is imaginary, it is also a big lie.

Suppose we agreed that whatever big lies the American nation has drawn upon are morally justified lies – Americans would still be in trouble. Myth can only do its inspirational work so long as it *not* recognized as myth. And for good or ill, the world we share with our children is one that insistently forces that recognition upon us. I doubt that revelations about Jefferson's liaison with a slave or evidence of Lincoln's racism provoke much surprise among today's high school students. The politics they see on the evening news, assuming that they pay it any heed, is too often a circus of greed, hypocrisy, and malice for patriotic innocence about the nation to develop far in their lives. Would it not be a great surprise to them if the politics of the past were very different from its often sordid present?

For most of their history, American schools could more or less easily obscure the mythic elements in the evolving patriotic narrative. Academic American history did not sharply and systematically diverges from patriotic history in the schools, and so the myth that children were taught could claim the legitimacy of impartial scholarship. Far more importantly, the political voices of those whom the narrative excluded from equal citizenship were still largely muted or inaudible. All this has changed. Academic American history has in recent decades developed in ways that discredit much within the traditional patriotic narrative. Slavery was not the benign, paternalistic institution it had been represented as for much of the twentieth century; it was oppression at its most terrible. And Emancipation did not signal the end of whatever wrong slavery had done; it was only one episode in a fitful and still far from complete struggle against American racism (Smith, 1997). These shifts in academic history mirror larger changes in the body politic that have come to seem irreversible. Formerly quiescent minorities clamor for equality and recognition and their most eloquent voices are commonly found within the academy. And the slow but inexorable demographic decline of white Americans to the status of one minority among others has begun to register in popular consciousness, making it harder for anyone to suppose that American identity could still be white identity.

Those of us who endorse multiculturalism will rightly be glad that a more honest history can now be taught in our schools. That history will acknowledge the immense contribution that many different people have made to the making of America. But will the new multicultural history teach a new patriotism? Gary Nash thinks so. Nash is among America's most distinguished historians. He has also contributed enormously to the improvement of history education in American schools. According to Nash, the teaching of multicultural history does not replace patriotism with something else; it signals rather the transition from an older patriotism, skewed by the prejudices of an Anglo elite, to a new, more egalitarian version that honors all those who have made America what it is today (Nash et al., 2000).

Multicultural history explores the past from the many disparate perspectives of those whose lives were invisible in the old patriotic story of great men, great wars, and ceaseless moral progress. We now have history from the bottom-up as well as from the top-down – the history of the poor as well as the rich, women as well as men. But even these distinctions are far too simple – the America experienced by immigrant women was not the same regardless of where they came from or where they went, and being black and female has never been the same as being white and female, and so on. And these categories too will lose their seeming unity under close scrutiny as differences within any one of them come into sharper focus. So perspectives proliferate, and as they do, the availability of *any* overarching national story might seem increasingly elusive.

Nash is aware of this difficulty, and in an interpretive sketch of the American Revolution he tries to show how new historical scholarship provides a far more complicated, conflict-ridden, but still patriotic interpretation of the beginnings of the republic. The Revolution was a matter of multiple struggles for liberty, according to Nash, some of which were tragic failures. "Black Americans joined with white (i.e., British) allies to expose the contradiction between resistance to British oppression and the reality of slavery." The Indians who gained nothing for fighting demonstrated "their continuing desires to secure the life, liberty, and the pursuit of happiness that the new republic proclaimed." And in Abigail Adam's spat with her husband John Adams on the alleged evils of patriarchal authority, Nash detects the first stirrings of a process that would eventually lead to "suffrage and equitable legal treatment for women" (Nash et al., 2000, pp. 84–86). In a word, the Revolution was a struggle for freedom in which all Americans were participants in one way or another, even if freedom for some came at the cost of subjection for others.

I am no historian, and I am so foolish as to challenge Gary Nash's scholarship. But Nash's confidence that this exemplifies a new patriotic history seems doubtful to me for reasons that have nothing to do with his expertise as an historian. First, the history of any oppressed people anywhere is about the struggle for freedom, or when freedom seems too remote even as an object of hope, the story is about the struggle of people to relieve as best they can the burden of their oppression. American history is not distinctive in his regard. And Nash's thumbnail sketch of the Revolution includes far too many who were denied liberty for anyone to infer that a principled antipathy to oppression was its driving force. Nash would almost certainly agree. Why then should the interpretive frame of liberty for all that he commends for a multicultural history of America conduce to a new American patriotism? Nash's answer is intimated in what he says about the "contradiction" between the moral high ground of free and equal citizenship on which the colonists staked their claims and the oppression in which the same colonists were so deeply involved (Nash et al., 2000, p. 86). The leitmotiv of the new patriotic history thus becomes the exalted values of free and equal citizenship at the constitutional core of civic identity, the betrayals to which the ideals have been subject, and the many ongoing struggles to make them real in the lives of all citizens.

I think this takes us close to the truth about the democratic patriotism we need in a multicultural nation but not quite close enough. The problem is that by itself the interpretive frame Nash wants our children to adopt might as easily carry one to civic apathy or despair as it does to engaged, democratic citizenship. For history to nourish patriotic engagement there must be powerful reason for students to believe that the "contradiction" between ideals and reality is not so great and immoveable that it divests their citizenship of any real meaning. But on that issue academic American history in its current state does *not* speak with a uniformly encouraging voice, and so simply by saying that the new multicultural history will teach patriotism as potent as the old seems a bit complacent. The fact that the old history taught a big, bad lie that no one can believe any more does not mean that a multicultural history told without the lies will give us another better, patriotism. In fact, whether a nation bereft of myth is possible at all is an open question, as Ernst Renan suggested over a century ago.

Consider a recent dispute on the pages of the *Journal of American History*. Gary Gerstle, a respected labor historian at the University of Maryland, responds to an article by David Hollinger, the author of a justly celebrated and cautiously optimistic book on the future of American nationhood. Hollinger's article was a response to an earlier critique by Gerstle:

> Hollinger criticizes me for neglecting the distinction between his description of the past, which is full of coercion and limitation, and his "normative" outline of the future, in which he imagines an America free of such constraints. But the confusion is not mine, but his; *if the past has been so coercive, then why should the future be so different? . . . Our history suggests that building a national community depends on repression and exclusion.* (Gerstle, 1997, p. 575, my italics)

For anyone who has been paying a little attention to the social sciences and humanities on US campuses in recent years this has a familiar ring to it. It is familiar *not* because it is at all typical of discourse in the humanities and social sciences; it is merely a currently chic species within the genus of academic arrogance and vanity. The scholar strikes the pose of the righteous and utterly assured moral judge of the national past, present, and future. (I suspect that the pose is one of the stranger mutations of that venerable American archetype – the sanctimonious Puritan preacher.) And he has bad news. The past was awful, the present is just as bad, and so too will be the future. Other people (i.e., rival scholars) are just insufficiently righteous or smart to see it.

This is antipatriotic history with a vengeance. To accept Gerstle's high-minded hopelessness is to give up on the very idea of building a national community. But to give up on that is necessarily to give up on building a *democratic* national community as well. To be sure, Gerstle might regard democracy as a very good thing. Still, consistency would require him to say that the only authentic democracy for Americans could be practiced in a "post-national" America, in which building democracy together has been abandoned. That is to say, groups who have been victimized by oppression should no longer seek to sustain any common "imagined community" of self-rule with groups who have been responsible for their oppression. The American state might continue to exist. But for all who have abjured the nation it would be no instrument of a common democratic community; it would be a site for struggling to gain power against those who would exploit one's group for their own ends. This would indeed be one kind of multicultural America: "difference" would be the victor over "sameness," and no one who is not white and male would succumb to the evil intent lurking behind all appeals to a shared American patria.

But who is likely to fare well or badly in this post-national America? If ethno-racial minorities and other traditionally oppressed groups forswear any common national identity with other Americans, the latter must reciprocate. For the nation depends on *common* imaginings, and if a large part of what has so far been a nation decides it wants none of it anymore, the rest simply cannot go on as before. Yet if there were no American nation, on what basis might one expect things to get better for those who were treated the worst when there was one? Asymmetries of power would not be undone merely by agreeing that no one should expect justice from the state. And no one could rationally suppose that the sense of justice among culturally and economically privileged Americans that was, according to Gerstle, always so feebly evident when there was a shared nation would suddenly blossom once there is none. So I shall charitably assume that Gerstle makes no such supposition. Perhaps he thinks it will at least be more difficult for the traditional oppressors to exploit people who were once co-nationals when they are that no longer. But that is scarcely less obtuse. The ease with which powerful states have always been able to abuse relatively weak and poor national minorities suggests that nothing is to be gained by forfeiting common nationhood.

That being so, to find someone as tough-minded as Gary Gerstle being such a dewy-eyed utopian when it comes to pondering the end of common American nationhood – assuming that he ponders it at all – is somewhat surprising. The end of a shared sense of nationhood would merely destroy a fragile bond of common belonging, and along with it, the possibility of any use that bond might have as an instrument for political change toward justice. I doubt that esteemed scholars at major research universities have much to worry about in a post-national America, but others might have much to fear.

I do not want to suggest that looking honestly at a demythologized national past will always corrode patriotism, much less plunge our children into Gerstle's odd state of political cynicism and naïveté. But the truth does not always edify us, in history or anywhere else. Perhaps very few American historians would see American nation-building through as dark a lens as Gary Gerstle. What his extreme case shows, however, is that multicultural American history is apt to be a less reliable vehicle of patriotic enthusiasm than Nash supposes. A demythologized American past reveals no heartening tale of steady moral progress by the very standards that Nash's interpretive frame of liberty for all would offer.

For many children, multicultural history might elicit the sense that the nation is not something worthy of any civic passion, despite the best intentions of multicultural teachers or textbook writers. Too many evils have been done in its name, and too many struggles have wasted lives for ideals that have often been proclaimed but never more than very imperfectly realized. Perhaps the best thing to do is to live in disregard of the nation. Prudence and respect for others will make one law-abiding, and many opportunities to help people in need will be open that have nothing to do with the grand idea of nationhood. Taking these opportunities will reliably bring tangible benefits to others' lives. Goodwill will not be wasted in political struggles that always yield less than they seem to promise and often come to an end in sheer failure. Volunteering at an AIDS hospice or at a resource center for immigrants may be a much better bet for decent people who want their decency to make a difference than volunteering to help someone win an election.

Contrary to critics on the right, the worry I express here is not about a new multicultural balkanization. If the best multicultural history shows anything, it is that America has always been rather more balkanized than many of its citizens would care to admit, and if one wishes to look for recent agents of balkanization, those who have thwarted the desegregation of American schools and isolated the inner cities must carry a vastly greater burden of responsibility than a few intemperate Afrocentrists. Blaming serious multicultural scholars and teachers for balkanizing the nation is an egregious case of shooting the messenger. My worry is altogether different. It is that multicultural history in our schools might easily contribute to the very processes of political demoralization that already threaten American democracy.

The public institutions of a democratic community can be destabilized in more than one way. Madison's worry that they could succumb to the mischief of factions is the one that has traditionally preoccupied Americans. But another possibility is that escalating cynicism and disengagement rather than factional passions could undo a common democratic community. People would increasingly cease to imagine themselves as part of such a community, retreating instead into whatever groups give them a sense of meaningful personal belonging.

4.3   Patriotic History and Democratic Idealism

At this point we might seem to be at an impasse. On the one hand, American citizens need to understand their nation's history as multicultural. Yet the narratives that constitute their multicultural history are too morally complicated reliably to inspire, and in some instances too shameful to warrant anything other than revulsion. Heroes lose their God-like status and become richly ambiguous and often opaque human beings, just like the rest of us, admirable in some ways but as often appalling in others. No linear pattern of democratic progress is discernible over time, or at least many will reasonably believe there is none. A democratic patriotism would seem at best a precarious achievement under these circumstances. On the other hand, the loss of all sense of common nationhood could only harm those who have suffered most from exclusionary ideals of civic identity that prevailed unchallenged in the past and cast long shadows on the present and future. A post-national America holds no prospect of giving them the justice and recognition they seek.

My point is not that democratic patriotism and multicultural history are irreconcilable and one can only be chosen if the other is renounced. Reconciliation is possible, indeed necessary. But it will be fragile. Americans should expect some abiding tension in their children's lives between the history they need to know and the patriots they need to become. All are better prepared to live with that tension as students, teachers, and citizens by acknowledging it openly rather than trying to evade it. I suspect that students will in general be grateful for their teachers' and parents' candor about this tension, and resistant to adults who would seek to disguise it by insisting that once we study American history in the light of recent scholarship it will arouse a patriotic spirit.

But where is the source of that reconciliation? The declaration that it is possible does not make it so. Perhaps the possibility of a patriotic history in a multicultural America has less to do with what students *find* when they study the past than with what they *bring* to their study. After all, the data of history – the documents and artifacts out of which we try to make sense of the past – do not themselves compel a democratic faith. They may often reveal truths that defeat our expectations or complicate our pieties, but they cannot establish the necessity of our ideals. What must be brought then to the venture of patriotic history is a distinctive political morality that insists on freedom and equality for all within a democratic community where citizens are respected in their cultural particularity within limits fixed by norms of mutual respect and civility. That politico-moral perspective does not properly operate as a filter in historical study, pushing disturbing facts into the background as a new patriotic myth crystallizes in the foreground. Its rightful function is to help students to understand their responsibilities as future citizens in a democracy whose character they cannot understand save through history. Only through history can they come to know how civic ideals can be enacted and betrayed in the messy, morally ambiguous world of the nation-state whose future they inherit. There is no "presentism" in this perspective because, as Nash rightly points out, these ideals directly link the present to the proclaimed civic self-understanding American civic inheritance, even if the best has been commonly obscured by the worst. And the "contradiction" between ideal and reality is no reason for apathy or disengagement for those learning to understand their civic responsibilities through the lens of democratic virtue. A mature democratic idealism carries no fond hope that the world is a place where ideal and reality easily join together. And the value of imperfect, even fleeting democratic achievement compels one to stay the course rather than give up on struggles that are as old as the nation itself.

If our students have come to identify with the morality of free and equal citizenship and the democratic community in which they belong, they will be disturbed by past and present failures of the American nation to keep faith with the ideals that constitute that morality. But then they will have no more reason to give up on democratic patriotism than children who have learned to be compassionate when they discover that the world contains many cruel people.

References

Anderson, B. (1991). *Imagined communities: Reflections on the origins and spread of nationalism*, rev. ed. London: Verso.

Gerstle, G. (1997). The power of nation. *The Journal of American History*, 85, 575–580.

Nash, G. B., Crabtree, C., & Dunn, R. E. (2000). *History on trial: Culture wars and the teaching of the past*, 2nd ed. New York: Vintage.

Renan, E. ([1882] 1992). What is a nation?. In H. Bhaba (Ed.), *Nation and narration*. London: Routledge.

Rhea, J. T. (1997). *Race pride and American identity*. Cambridge, MA: Harvard University Press.

Smith, R. (1997). *Civic ideals: Conflicting visions of citizenship in US history*. New Haven, CT: Yale University Press.

Zimmerman, J. (2000). Each "race" could have its heroes sung: Ethnicity and the history wars in the 1920s. *The Journal of American History*, 87, 92–111.

Chapter 5
Racism: What It Is and What It Isn't[1]

Lawrence Blum

Abstract Productive conversations about racial matters are too infrequent, both inside and outside classroom settings. Confusion about the meaning of "racism" contributes to the problem, and some guidelines will help. First, within a given category (actions, jokes, stereotypes, remarks, stereotypes, persons), we should confine "racism" to especially egregious wrongs in that category. Not every racial stereotype is racist. Not every racially insensitive action is a racist action. The distinct opprobrium attached to racism and racist can be retained and protected if we recognize that racism refers to racial inferiorization or racial antipathy, and that the different categorical forms of racism can all be related to either of those two definitions. Second, we should not confuse racism in one category with racism in another. A person who is prey to a racist stereotype is not necessarily "a racist"; nor does he or she necessarily operate from racist motives. Finally, racism by no means captures all of what can go wrong in the domain of race. There is a much larger terrain of moral ills in the racial domain than racism itself, and we should draw on our manifold linguistic resources – racial insensitivity, failure to recognize racial identity, racial ignorance, racial anxiety, racial injustice, racial homogenization, and so on – to express and describe moral disvalue in this domain.

We in the United States are notoriously poor at communicating about racial matters. David Shipler, in his informative and insightful book *A Nation of Strangers*, rightly says, "Blacks and whites do not listen well to each other (Shipler, 1997, p. 447). Native Americans, Latinos, Chicanos, and Asian-Americans are not all that much better. We find honest discussion about race *across racial lines* especially difficult. Ironically, race is the subject of scores of books and articles. And one often hears impatience expressed about race. "Race is talked to death," it is said.

There may be a lot of words written about race. But there is a good deal less honest, open, and productive conversation about it among persons of different races

Lawrence Blum
University of Massachusetts Boston

[1] Much of the material in this lecture is drawn from chapters 1 and 3 of my book, *"I'm Not a Racist, But. . ."*: *The Moral Quandary of Race* (Blum, 2002).

than there needs to be. For the past several years I have taught courses on race and racism to undergraduates, graduate students in education, and high school students. Most of my classes were quite racially and ethnically diverse. In my experience a range of reasons accounts for the lack of productive conversation. People are afraid of giving offense. They are afraid of revealing prejudices that they know are not socially acceptable. They are afraid of *appearing* prejudiced, even if they are actually not. They feel ignorant of groups other than their own and are afraid to take the risk of revealing their ignorance and trying to remedy it. The whole idea of "race" just carries unpleasant associations with them, and they would rather avoid it. They may think we should all be "color-blind," that it is somehow wrong even to take notice of, or make reference to, other people's racial identity. This idea of color blindness is both particularly strong, yet also particularly misplaced, among teachers, especially at the precollege level. Teachers can not serve their students fully unless they are aware of the full range of factors affecting their lives, and race is very likely to be one of those factors (Schofield, 1989).

Some reasons for reluctance to engage in race discussions are more race-specific. Blacks, and to a lesser extent other people of color, may want to avoid having to deal with what they assume will be offensive or at least annoying remarks from others. Or they might not want to have to be in a position of correcting others' (especially whites') ignorance. Latinos, Native Americans, and Asian-Americans may not be certain how to insert themselves into a discourse which seems to them dominated by "black/white" issues, or they may feel resentful of this dominance, and assume their specific concerns will not be adequately attended to. Notwithstanding these obstacles, I have also found a great deal of goodwill among students, and an anxious desire for their teachers to create contexts that do manage to facilitate constructive interracial interchange.

Each of the cited obstacles is deserving of further attention. However, I wish in this lecture to focus on a different obstacle, though one that bears on several of those just mentioned. It is the idea of "racism" itself. There is a great deal of confusion surrounding the meaning of "racism" and "racist." Yet one thing is clear – few people wish to be, or to be thought of as racists. Fear of being thought racist, together with a good deal of confusion as to what it is that being racist consists in, is a potent formula for inhibition regarding discussing racial matters, most especially for whites who are, understandably, in most danger of being thought to be, and indeed of actually being, racist.

Clarifying meanings is the professional task of the philosopher, and I think that if we become clearer about what "racism" actually consists in, and what lies outside of the scope of racism yet may still be morally problematic, we will be better equipped to engage in productive discussions about race. Of course I have no illusions that merely clarifying meanings will bring about either racial justice or racial harmony, or even the more minimal goal of producing helpful conversations about these matters. But it seems an essential first step.

The words "racism" and "racist" have become deeply entrenched in the moral vocabulary of the United States and Western Europe. "Is television a racist institution?" asks an article concerning the National Association for the Advancement of Colored People (NAACP) criticizing the fall 1999 prime-time network shows for having no "minority" actors in lead roles in 27 new series (Weinraub, 1999, pp. A1, A14). Blacks who criticized other blacks for supporting a white over a black candidate in a mayoral race were called racist. A white girl in Virginia said that it was racist for an African-American teacher in her school to wear African attire (Shipler, 1997, p. 92). The Milton, Wisconsin, school board voted to retire its "Redmen" name and logo depicting a Native American wearing a headdress, because they have been criticized as being racist. Racist has become the standard way to condemn and deplore people, actions, policies, symbols, and institutions for malfeasance in the racial domain.

In serving as a term of moral reproach, racism has joined more time-honored vices such as "dishonesty," "cruelty," "cowardice," and "hypocrisy." Apart from a small number of avowed white supremacists, most Americans wish very much to avoid being called racist. In this regard, "racist" operates similarly to "cruel." Few admit to being cruel. Persons who are cruel might say the target of their cruelty deserved it; or they might simply fail to recognize the harm caused by their actions. Similarly, no one admits to being racist. Those who are, or are thought to be, might say their remarks were just a joke; they did not intend any harm; people are just being oversensitive; it was a personal, not a racial, thing; and the like. One expects people who are accused of being racist to deny it; newspapers should stop regarding this as newsworthy.

5.1 Overusing "Racism"

Yet the widely shared reproach carried by "racist" is threatened by a current tendency to overuse the term. Some feel that the word is thrown around so much that anything involving "race" that someone does not like is liable to castigation as racist – for example, merely mentioning someone's race (or racial designation),[2] using the word "Oriental" for Asians without recognizing its origins and its capacity for insult, or socializing only with members of one's own racial group. Many people would not agree, or would not be sure, that *any* of these, or the four examples in the paragraph before the previous one, constitute racism. A few observers go even further and suspect that the word has lost all significant meaning. "Racism is … what black activists define it to be. … When words lose coherent meaning, they also lose the power to shame. 'Racism,' 'sexism,' and 'homophobia' have become such words. Labels that should horrify are simply shrugged off" (Nuechterlein, 1996, p. B9). *Time* columnist Lance Morrow sees social damage in this same development: "The words 'racism' and 'racist' are a feckless indulgence, corrosive to blacks and whites alike and to relations between them" (Morrow, 1996, p. 18).

---

[2] I do not believe that there are races in the sense in which "race" is generally understood in popular discourse, so I regard it as misleading to say that someone "is of a certain race." It is more accurate to say that someone has, or has been assigned, a racial designation, or that she is a member of a racial group; I will generally use the latter expression.

A major reason for what Robert Miles calls the "conceptual inflation" (Miles, 1989, pp. 41–68) to which the idea of racism has been subject is its having become the central or even only notion used to mark morally suspect behavior, attitude, and social practice regarding race. The result – either something is racist, or it is morally in the clear. In Boston a white police officer, as a bizarre joke and apparently with no malice intended, placed a hangman's noose on the motorcycle of a black police officer. "Police probe sees no racism in noose prank," says the headline of an article reporting the findings of an investigation into the incident. Perhaps the white officer was not a racist, nor operating from racist motives; but, as the victim in the incident said, "You cannot hang a noose like that near any black man who knows his history and say it does not have tremendous significance" (*Boston Globe*, 1999, p. B1).[3] If our only choices are to label an act "racist" or "nothing to get too upset about," those who seek to garner moral attention to some racial malfeasance will be tempted to call it racist. That overuse in turn feeds a diminishing of racism's moral force, and thus contributes to weakened concern about racism and other racial ills.

Not all rac*ial* incidents are rac*ist* incidents. Not every instance of racial conflict, insensitivity, discomfort, miscommunication, exclusion, injustice, or ignorance should be called racist. This more varied and nuanced moral vocabulary needs to be more fully utilized, complementing racist and racism. All forms of racial ills should elicit concern from responsible citizens. If someone displays racial insensitivity, but not racism, people should be able to see that straightforwardly as a matter of moral concern. In a soccer game, a nine-year-old white boy said "Boy, pass the ball over here" to one of his black teammates, and "was virtually accused of being a racist by the father of one of his teammates," says an article on the incident. (That description may itself reflect the newspaper's loss of an evaluative vocabulary other than "racist" and "racism," rather than what the black boy's father actually said.) In any case, the white boy was almost surely not a racist and the article itself goes on to express more accurately the racial ill involved in his remark: "The word 'boy' is a tripwire attached to so much charged racial baggage that it is no longer safely used as a term for a prepubescent male."

If a policy has a racially unjust effect, or unequally affects already unequally placed racial groups, this too should be reason for concern, even if there is no suggestion that it arises from racist motives, nor is part of the sort of entrenched pattern strongly rooted in historical racism. For example, school lunch programs have been criticized for relying too strongly on milk, in light of the African-Americans' substantial propensity toward lactose intolerance; but no untoward motives, or failures of sensitivity, need have prompted the original policies favoring milk for them to be of concern. Similarly, it is troubling if prime-time TV fails adequately to reflect its viewers', and the society's, ethno-racial diversity; but it is not necessarily "racist."[4] Someone who exhibits a culpable

---

[3]The black officer seemed clearly to be referring to lynching.

[4]It is noteworthy that it was the newspaper article, rather than the NAACP itself, that called the networks "racist," or framed the issue as one of racism. Kweisi Mfume, the president of the NAACP, said only that the programming was "a virtual whitewash." *New York Times*, September 20, 1999, p. A1.

ignorance about racial matters bearing on an interaction with an acquaintance or coworker should feel a degree of shame about this, and be motivated to correct that ignorance – without him or her having to think he or she has been racist. We should not be faced with the choice of "racism or nothing."

Racism's conceptual inflation and moral overload can arise from a another source as well – designating as "racism" any prejudice, injustice, domination, inferiorizing, bigotry, and the like against human groups defined in *any* manner, for example, by gender, disability, or nationality. In *The Decent Society*, Avishai Margalit, an Israeli philosopher, discusses racism as the denying of dignity to *any human group*, and uses as a particular test case "retarded" persons (Margalit, 1996, pp. 80–83). This inflated use of racism pays indirect tribute to the centrality of racism as a form of oppression and denial of dignity in contemporary Western consciousness. That centrality is reflected also in later coinages, such as "sexism," "ableism" (discrimination against the disabled), "classism," and "heterosexism" – all consciously modeled on "racism," and attempting to draw on racism's moral opprobrium to condemn other phenomena seen as in important ways analogous to racism.[5] This racism-influenced proliferation of other "isms" at least avoids the confusion wrought by Margalit's conflating all of them with racism itself. At least it encourages us to explore the similarities between discrimination, exploitation, and denials of dignity based on race, and those based on other human attributes, such as gender, sexual orientation, disability, national membership, and the like, thereby allowing the possibility of significant *disanalogies*. Margalit's subsuming all these moral ills under racism cuts off that inquiry at the starting line, and, in so doing, contributes to a counterproductive inflation of the term "racism."

5.2 Racist Jokes and Racist Persons

A different source of confusion and moral overload regarding racism concerns what one might call racism's location. Many different kinds of entity can be racist – actions, institutions, practices, symbols, statements, jokes, persons, to name a few. The moral significance of an attribution of racism differs depending on its location. Take racist jokes for instance. A person who tells a racist joke is not necessarily a racist, in the sense of a person who harbors pervasive racial animosity or inferiorizing attitudes toward a racially defined group. He may tell the joke without sharing the racist sentiments the joke expresses. People often tell jokes as a way of trying to win acceptance; they might tell whatever they think will bring a laugh. Imagine, for example, someone telling a joke that makes fun of Asian-Americans in a particularly

---

[5] Of those listed, only "sexism" has fully succeeded in attaching moral condemnation to its referent – discrimination against, or the denial of dignity to, women, or discrimination on the basis of sex in general – in popular thought and speech.

demeaning manner, in order to gain acceptance in a group. (The group could consist of any ethno-racial group, except Asian-Americans. I am not assuming that only whites tell racist jokes [or are racists, for that matter].[6]) This individual does not necessarily hold racist views of Asians or Asian-Americans. The joke is racist, but the teller of the joke is not.

Of course, this does not mean that, as long as one does not share the racist views a joke expresses, it is perfectly fine to tell such a joke. To think that it is all right is to reason in precisely the all-or-nothing manner I have been criticizing. It is a very bad thing to tell a racist joke. One often hears public figures who have been caught out telling a racist joke or making a racist remark defending themselves by saying that they did not intend any offense to the group in question, that they are not racist. Often this defense is quite disingenuous, and the individual in fact does hold the racist attitudes implied in the joke. But even when it is not, this is a feeble defense from a moral point of view. It is bad to tell a racist joke, whether one means to offend, or holds racist attitudes, or not.

Jokes, and humor more generally, raise a common locational issue about racism – the difference between intention and effect – illustrated in two examples of racist humor that came to public attention in the late 1990s. One was a fraternity party, in which the fraternity members dressed up in Native-American-warrior attire and wielded tomahawks. A second, again a fraternity, involved staging a mock slave auction. In both cases, members of the fraternities in question defended themselves by saying that they did not mean to offend anyone. But the moral shortcoming in both cases did not lie in setting out to deliberately demean Native Americans and African-Americans. It lay in the fraternity members failing to realize that what they were doing *was* demeaning to Native Americans and African-Americans, whether they *intended* this or not. It is not even clear that ignorance of the affront would be morally more acceptable than an intention to affront.

Still, engaging in racist humor does not make one a racist. More generally, clarity and racial understanding would be advanced if people attempted to take greater care in locating the racism they allege in a situation. Is it a practice that is racist, whether the persons who participate in the practice are racist or not? Is it the motive of an act that is racist? Is it an attitude taken to be expressed in a remark, or the remark itself? Is it a person about whom one knows enough to say that he or she is "a racist?"

To help us avoid the first form of confusion about racism – conceptual inflation – I will suggest a core meaning rooted in the history of its use, that confines "racism" to phenomena deserving of the severest moral condemnation (within the appropriately located type, that is, act, statement, joke, person, and so on). Fixing on such a definition should encourage us to make use of the considerable other resources our language affords us for describing and evaluating race-related ills that do not characteristically rise to the level of racism – racial insensitivity, racial con-

---

[6] In *"I'm Not a Racist, But. . ."* I argue that members of any group can be racist. For instance, I counter the view that only whites can be racist because only whites hold power as a racial group.

flict, racial injustice, racial ignorance, racial discomfort, and others. Such an agreed-upon meaning for racism should facilitate interracial communication, at least in diminishing a free-floating and pervasive fear of the dreaded charge of racism – by making clearer what is and what is not to be counted as racism – while at the same time encouraging a wider scope of moral concern to race-related phenomena. In doing so, my suggested definition of racism should stanch the creeping loss of moral cachet of the term "racism" itself, with its attendant undermining of moral concern toward racism and other race-related ills.

5.3   Defining "Racism"

In proffering a definition of racism, it would be folly to claim that one was doing no more than articulating "our concept" of racism. Even apart from inflationary usages, it is not likely that all employments of that concept cohere in an overall, self-consistent whole. Nevertheless, especially in light of the history of this concept, I hope my proposal can reasonably be viewed as a plausible candidate for a core meaning.

"Racism" was first used by German social scientists in the 1930s to refer to the ideology of race superiority central to Nazism, and its core historical meaning broadened out to other systems of racial domination and oppression, such as segregation, South African apartheid, and European colonialism. In this light, I want to suggest that all forms of racism can be related to either of two general "themes" – *inferiorization* and *antipathy*. Inferiorizing is treating the racial other as inferior or of lesser value and, secondarily, viewing the racial other as inferior. Racial antipathy is simply a strong dislike, often tinged with hostility, toward individuals or groups because of their race. Of the two modes, inferiorization is more obviously linked to historical racist doctrines and social systems. Slavery, segregation, imperialism, apartheid, and Nazism all involved certain groups being regarded and treated as inferior to other groups.

But race-based hatred was also central to the ideological and attitudinal components of Nazism, and, for whatever reason, racial bigotry, hostility, and hatred are now securely linked to the contemporary idea of racism in both Europe and the United States. Indeed, the racial bigot is many people's paradigm image of "a racist," and few would now deny application of the appellation "racist" to such persons. A disturbing but illuminating example of contemporary antipathy racism occurred in Washington State in 1999. The Makah tribe of the Olympic Peninsula announced its intention to hunt for whales as a way of instilling pride and tradition in the tribe's youth. The hunt was permitted by the government, and the tribe killed a whale in May of that year. Many non-Native American Washington residents were outraged by this act. Amidst arguably reasonable objections to the whale hunting were expressions of outright antipathy racism toward the Makah, and toward Native Americans more generally. One letter to the *Seattle Times*, for example, said, "I have a very real hatred for Native Americans now. It's embarrassing, but I would be lying if I said it wasn't the truth" (Tizon, 1999).

Inferiorizing and antipathy racism are distinct. Some superiority racists do not hate the target of their beliefs. They may have a paternalistic concern and feelings of kindness for persons they regard as their human inferiors. This form of racism was prevalent among slave owners, and characterized many whites' views of blacks during the segregation era in the United States. The concern and kindness are misdirected, and demeaning, because the other is not seen as an equal, or even as a full human being; it is a racist form of concern. Nevertheless such attitudes are distinct from antipathy and hatred.

On the other side, not every race hater regards the target of her hatred as inferior. In the U.S. antipathy toward Asians and Jews often accompanies, and is in part driven by, a kind of resentment of those seen as in some ways superior (e.g., more successful). And some whites who hate blacks do not really regard blacks as inferior; they may fear them and be hostile to them, but fear and hostility are not the same as contempt and other forms of inferiorizing. (Again, antipathy and contempt may accompany one another.) Survey research suggests that pure superiority racism toward blacks has substantially decreased since segregation, more so than hostility-based racism (Schuman et al., 1997, pp. 156–157). Nevertheless, the great and persistent racial inequalities in our society provide a standing encouragement to advantaged groups to see disadvantaged groups as somehow deserving their lower status.

However, antipathy and inferiorizing racism are not entirely separate either. The paternalistic inferiorizing racist (e.g., a white segregationist) often hates those members of the racial group who do not accept the inferior social position he regards as appropriate to their inferior natures – for example, blacks who do not engage in the deference behavior the paternalistic racist expects. Emmett Till was lynched in 1955 out of hatred directed toward a young black man who had transgressed the rules of racial deference and constraint defining him as an inferior being. In addition, many racists both hate *and* regard as inferior members of a particular racial group (and not only a particular subcategory of such members, such as those who do not "stay in their place").

5.4 Racial and Racist Stereotypes

If we confine racism to manifestations or representations of racial antipathy or racial inferiorizing, we can see that many things can go wrong in the area of race without being racist. Consider two objectionable stereotypes of blacks – blacks as intellectually deficient, and blacks as good dancers. The first is a straightforwardly racist stereotype; it portrays blacks as inferior in regard to a fundamental human attribute. The second, however, is not racist, on my account. It attributes a positive rather than a negative quality. It is a far less objectionable stereotype than the inferiority stereotype.

Nevertheless, the stereotype of blacks as good dancers is still objectionable. Like any stereotype, it wildly overgeneralizes about a group; it blinds us to the internal diversity of the group – some blacks are bad dancers, some are good, some are so-

so (and this is so of every racial group). Also, all stereotyping discourages recognizing the individuality of members of the group.

The stereotype of blacks as good dancers is also objectionable in a more specific, historically contextual sense, which can be recognized in the more variegated moral vocabulary revealed by loosening our fixation on racism and racist. This stereotype hearkens back to the slave era, when viewing blacks as good dancers was bound up with their being seen as mentally inferior. While this direct implication is no longer clearly attached to the "good dancer" stereotype, stereotypes must be viewed historically as well as contemporarily, and a given stereotype's resonance with a much more distinctly racist stereotype renders it objectionable in a way that stereotypes without such historical resonance would not be. Other stereotypes lacking such historical resonance are, for example, Asians as poor drivers, blacks as poor swimmers, and whites as not being able to jump. All are objectionable, racial (race-based) stereotypes. But it is moral overload to call them *racist* stereotypes, and to do so contributes to a cheapening of the moral force of the idea of racism.

5.5   Racial Discomfort or Anxiety

Another application of the proposed definition of racism is the difference between racial antipathy and what I will call "racial discomfort" or "racial anxiety." Consider the following example.

Ms. Verano is a white fourth-grade teacher. She feels comfortable with all the children in her very racially mixed class. She holds all students to equally high standards of performance. But, though she has never admitted this to herself, she is not really comfortable with most of the black parents. She does not dislike blacks, nor does she think they are inferior. However, she is not particularly familiar with African-American culture, knows very few blacks other than her students, and is not confident about her ability to communicate with black adults. As a result Ms. Verano is somewhat defensive when speaking with black parents in parent conferences, and is not able to listen to their concerns and viewpoints about their children as well as she does with parents in other racial groups. Because she does not glean as much information from the black parents about their children as she does from the other parents, she is not able to serve these children as well as the other children in her class. Ms. Verano is not racist, on my view. She bears no antipathy toward blacks; I have built this feature into the example. Nor does she regard blacks as inferior. Ms. Verano's situation is best described by saying that she is uncomfortable with black adults (not children). She has "racial discomfort" or "racial anxiety."

Racial anxiety is quite common in the United States, especially, I believe, among whites, although it can be found in any racial group. Racial anxiety can stem from different sources, and one of them can be anxiety that one's racist prejudices be revealed. In such a case racial anxiety would be a manifestation of racism. However, racial anxiety is not always racist in its genesis. We can realize that a group of persons is different from us in some socially important way, and we can feel that we are just not knowledgeable enough about this group to feel comfortable in the presence of its members. We can be anxious that we will embarrass ourselves by saying or doing the "wrong thing." We may worry that the group will dislike or reject us if we attempt to approach it. This social anxiety is perfectly familiar regarding cultural differences; the individual is anxious approaching a culture about which he or she lacks knowledge. Members of different racial groups are also often quite ignorant of one another's modes of life (sometimes but not always because cultural and racial differences correspond), even if they interact in schools and workplaces. In a sense racial anxiety is even *more* likely than mere cultural anxiety, since differences in "race" are more socially charged than are cultural differences. If one is equally ignorant of the other group, there is more reason to be anxious that one will violate some unforeseen norm with regard to a racially different group than a culturally different one.

In itself, racial anxiety or discomfort is not racism. Nor is racial discomfort the sort of thing for which its possessor is subject to moral criticism. It is not morally bad to be racially anxious, as it *is* morally bad to be racially prejudiced. However, racial discomfort is still a bad thing, and an individual who recognizes his or her racial anxiety should not rest content with it just because it is not a moral blot on his or her character. This is so, in part, because, as in Ms. Verano's case, it can lead to acts of a discriminatory character; Ms. Verano is unlikely to be able to educate her black pupils to the same degree as she does her other students, since she will lack information pertinent to them.

In addition racial anxiety reinforces a sense of separateness and "otherness" concerning those of other racial groups. It makes it difficult to recognize internal diversity in such groups, and to appreciate the individuality of members of the group. It feeds into (in addition to drawing on) the homogenizing of racial groups that is a typical pitfall in the racial arena.

Racial discomfort is also inimical to the development of interracial community and other forms of productive interracial relationship. It inhibits a sense of identification across racial lines, and reinforces a sense (particularly found among high school and some college students) that it is somehow more "natural" to socialize with members of one's own racial group than of other groups. We should strive for a society in which people feel as comfortable as possible interacting in all public and private venues with members of ethnic and racial groups other than their own. Such comfort would not only make social existence more pleasant, varied, and interesting for members of all groups, but would serve the purposes of civic attachment and civic engagement as well. Teachers in a position to do so would do well to make an effort to decrease racial discomfort and anxiety in their classes, for example by forming interracial groups for various tasks, encouraging interracial communication, explicitly discussing its importance and pitfalls, and the like.[7] Individuals are well advised to look for signs of racial discomfort in themselves and, if they discover them, do what they can to relieve this discomfort, for example

---

[7] Stephan (1999) provides a wealth of information about how to improve intergroup relations in schools.

by reaching out to persons of other racial groups or by becoming more familiar with, and knowledgeable about, the modes of life of those groups.

Furthermore, the fact that it is generally difficult to tell whether reluctance to engage with racial others is a product of antipathy or mere discomfort itself takes a toll on racial minorities who have to worry and wonder about the source of some troubling racial interaction. " 'In waiting rooms or lobbies … I've tried to initiate a conversation [with whites], and I could tell they don't want to talk,' says Sharon Walter, an African-American. 'But when a white person walks in, conversation begins. 'I don't want to think it's racism … The better part of me wants to think otherwise.' " (Shipler, 1997, p. 448). Merely having such thoughts is itself a psychic cost.

In summary, then, racial anxiety or discomfort is not, in itself, racist (although it *can* be a manifestation of underlying racism). Yet it is still a bad thing, destructive to interracial relationships.

5.6   Race, Identity, and Recognition

Another race-related ill distinct from racism is illustrated in the following example. A Haitian-American girl is one of two black students in her class. When a race-related issue arises in discussion, the teacher turns to her and asks her what "the black point of view" is on the question at hand.

There seem several distinct though related wrongs this teacher has committed. He has failed to recognize Haitian-Americans as a distinct ethnic group within the larger "black" umbrella. He has treated a racial group in an overly homogeneous manner, implying that there could be something that could coherently be called "the black point of view" on an issue. Finally, he has failed to recognize the student as an individual, with her own individual views.

These three related forms of misrecognition are directed toward an individual or a group of which the individual is a member. The latter two – racial homogenization, and not acknowledging individuality – are particularly serious failings in a teacher. However, that is not to say that they are racist. The teacher's behavior need not imply that he harbors animus toward blacks, or regards them as inferior.

5.7   Racial Motives and Racial Stereotypes

Confusion about both the location and the meaning of racism infected public under standing of a particularly tragic event that took place in Providence, Rhode Island, in January 2000. Several women were fighting in a late-night diner. The night manager threw the patrons out of the diner, where some male friends got involved, one of whom drew a gun. Inside the diner, an off-duty patrolman, Cornel Young, Jr., an African-American, was waiting for a take-out order. Meanwhile, the police had been called to the scene outside. Officer Young, after warning the patrons to get down, rushed outside to help the two officers on the scene, his gun drawn. (Providence police are required to carry their firearms when off duty.)

The two officers had ordered the male friend to drop his gun, which he did, and they then turned to Officer Young and ordered him to do so as well. It is not clear whether Young heard the order, but in any case he did not comply, and the two officers, who were white, shot and killed him. It emerged that, despite the officers' failing to recognize Officer Young, one of the officers had been a police academy classmate of Young's, and both had graduated in the same class three years earlier.

The killing sparked community outrage and anguish. Charges of racism were made. It was said that the killing was "racially motivated." Eventually a federal civil rights investigation took place, and the two officers were cleared of having intended to deprive Officer Young of his civil rights, or of acting out of racial animosity.

It is impossible to know whether the two officers were racially biased against blacks. However, their behavior is perfectly consistent with their lacking any form of racial prejudice or racial motivation. It is not likely that they shot at Young because they disliked black people. Some people, recognizing this, then felt some relief. The incident turned from one involving racism to a (mere) "tragic accident."

But this response oversimplifies. Racism may be absent in motivations and attitudes but be present elsewhere. In this situation, it is much more plausible to think that it lay in the stereotypes that the officers carried in their minds about blacks. That is why, or part of why, they reacted to a black man with a gun in plainclothes as if he were a perpetrator, even though they actually knew him as a fellow officer. In another widely reported case around the same time, four white officers in New York City killed an innocent black man whom they wrongly took to be reaching for a gun. Treating blackness as if it were an indicator of suspiciousness or criminality is referred to as "racial profiling" and has come in for a good deal of public criticism as a result of these and similar incidents, not only ones involving fatalities.

The white officers who killed Officer Young were apparently genuinely remorseful and upset by their having unwittingly killed a fellow officer. But this does not mean they were not prey to racial stereotypes linking blackness to criminality. Officer Young's mother was surely correct when she said that her son would be unlikely to have been shot had he been white. But it is important to be careful about what we mean if we say that he was killed "because he was black." It does not necessarily mean "out of hostility or animosity toward black persons." It could mean "because he was seen in the moment as a dangerous person and this was so in part because he was black." I believe it is also plausible to refer to this racial stereotype as racist. But my point here is not so much to defend that position as to encourage clarity as to the location of what is, or was, racially objectionable in the situation. It was in the stereotype, not in the motives of the white officers. And it shows the tremendous danger that can accompany racist stereotypes even in the absence of racial antipathy; they can be life threatening.

I have given a stripped down version of this complex racial situation, and want to mention only two other points. First, some members of the community placed some of the blame on the Providence police department's failure to educate its police force about the dangers and wrong of racial stereotyping and racial profiling. That is, they saw the fault in a kind of institutional irresponsibility regarding race, in the context of a recognition that antiblack stereotypes are particularly troubling in a police force that is meant to be protectors of their community.

The second race-related matter is more speculative on my part. Even though the white officers, and especially the one who graduated from the police academy with Officer Young, knew him, it is possible that a form of racial homogenization was involved in their failure to recognize him. Perhaps the officer in some sense still saw all blacks, or black men, as "looking alike." Perhaps in the heat of the moment the image of blackness blocked his seeing Officer Young as an individual person. Racial thinking does, in general, inhibit the perception of others as individuals; the case of the teacher asking the black student for "the black point of view" would be another version of this same homogenization. Perhaps – again I am speculating – although the white officer did know Officer Young, whites and blacks did not interact much on or off the job; if so this social segregation might have contributed to the racial homogenization that in turn contributed to his failing to recognize Officer Young.

5.8   Conclusion

Gaining some clarity about what racism means will help us engage in productive conversations about racial matters – conversations that are too infrequent, both inside and outside classroom settings. We have seen three ways by which we might gain that clarity. First, within a given category (actions, jokes, stereotypes, remarks, stereotypes, persons), we should confine "racism" to especially egregious wrongs in that category. Not every racial stereotype is racist. Not every remark that is racially offensive is racist. Not every racially insensitive action is a racist action. I have suggested that the distinct opprobrium attached to racism and racist can be retained and protected if we recognize that racism refers to racial inferiorization or racial antipathy, and that the different categorical forms of racism can all be related to either of those two definitions.

Second, we should not confuse racism in one category with racism in another. A person who is prey to a racist stereotype is not necessarily a racist; nor does he or she necessarily operate from racist motives. A remark can be unquestionably racist without the person making the remark being a racist, or making the remark for a racist reason or motive.

Finally, in endeavoring to protect the distinct moral opprobrium of the accusation of racism from conceptual inflation and moral overload, as well as from categorical drift and confusion, we must at the same time recognize that racism by no means captures all of what can go wrong in the domain of race. There is a much larger terrain of moral ills in the racial domain than racism itself, and we should draw on our manifold linguistic resources – racial insensitivity, failure to recognize racial identity, racial ignorance, racial anxiety, racial injustice, racial homogenization, and so on – to express and describe moral disvalue in this domain. Moral concern is appropriately directed toward this wider domain, and should not be confined to racism appropriately so called.

References

Boston Globe (1999, April 29). Black, white officers cited in noose incident, p. B1.

Blum, L. (2002). *"I'm not a racist, but…": The moral quandary of race*. Ithaca, NY: Cornell University Press.

Margalit, A. (1996). *The decent society*. Cambridge, MA: Harvard University Press.

Miles, R. (1989). *Racism*. London: Routledge.

Morrow, L. (1996). *Time, b*[12/5/94] cited in *Extra!*, vol. 9, #2, March/April 1996.

Nuechterlein, J. (1996). *First Things*, August–September 1996, from *Chronicle of Higher Education*, September 6, 1996.

Schofield, J. W. 1989. *Black and white in school: Trust, tension, or tolerance*? New York: Teachers College Press.

Schuman, H., Steeh, C., Bobo, L., & Krysan, M. (1997). *Racial attitudes in America: Trends and interpretation*, rev. ed. Cambridge, MA: Harvard University Press.

Shipler, D. K. (1997). *A Country of strangers: Blacks and whites in America*. New York: Vintage Books.

Stephan, W. (1999). *Reducing prejudice and stereotyping in schools*. New York: Teachers College Press.

Tizon, A. (1999). Whale killing uncovers anti-Indian hatred (1999, May 30). *Boston Globe*.

Weinraub, B. (1999). Stung by criticism of fall shows, TV networks add minority roles (1999, September 20). *New York Times*.

Chapter 6
For Goodness Sake: How Religious Stories Work To Make Us Good and the Goodness that They Make[1]

Walter Feinberg

Abstract This essay examines the possible meanings of the claim that one needs to be religious to be a moral person in order to determine whether there is any sense in which it could be true. It concludes that the claim has a number of different possible meanings but only one suggests a uniquely religious conception of morality. The chapter then draws out some implications for moral education.

6.1 Introduction

Today I want to talk about stories, the way in which they make us good and the kind of goodness that they make. I am not talking about any stories, but about ones familiar to us all. I am talking about stories that have been along for a very long time stories about temptation, jealousy, murder, friendships, love, executions, sacrifice, and forgiveness; stories about floods, wars, persecution. The box office appeal of the stories I have in mind would make the most successful Hollywood director drool with envy. These are stories that have been heard again and again by more than half the world and the royalties on the retellings alone would make their authors rich unto the hundredth generation. Yet, not only have these stories been read more times than any other literature, but they have been banned more than any other as well. In America they can be told by anyone to anyone, but the spaces in which they are told have been the subject of constitutional debates and Supreme Court decisions. Yet the stories are so well known that one only needs to glimpse a small fragment for the emotion of the whole to be evoked.

To some, these stories are more important than a balanced diet. If our children grow up without these stories, it is feared that they will lose their moral bearings. Children who grow up without glimpsing daily story fragments, without evoking

Walter Feinberg
The University of Illinois

[1] A version of this talk was presented for the Villemain Lecture at San Jose State University in Winter, 2003. My appreciation to Michael Katz and the Villemain Lecture Committee for the invitation. The work here has been supported by the Spencer Foundation

the emotions that the whole story seeks to evoke, will not grow up to be complete adults – they will be devoid of full membership in a complete community, a community that includes a spiritual dimension. Without prayer, without a visual reminder of God's commandments, without the words to remind our children of the whole, they will be forever lost.

Indeed, the philosopher Alasdair MacIntyre (1988, pp. 326–349) rejects liberalism as a viable philosophy because of the poverty of its stories, extolling in its place the tradition of Saint Thomas because of its wealth of stories. MacIntyre of course overstates the point. As if one who read only Saint Thomas and not the Bible came away thinking that Christianity had no good stories, only dry philosophy and legalisms about the findings of natural law. So the MacIntyre point about liberalism fits those who have only Hobbs, Locke, Kant Mills, Dewey, and Rawls without ever reading Twain, Hawthorne or Whitman, or Harding. True, the biblical tradition has more pungent short stories, but the authors of liberal fiction perfected the novel.

Nevertheless, putting this quibble aside, MacIntyre could be right in emphasizing the importance of stories and their influence in raising children with a certain understanding of goodness. Yet for religion it is not the story alone that is important, it is the story in context, its place, that makes a difference as well. Here I want to talk about these stories and about one of the places in which their telling is legitimized in American society – religious, and specifically religious schools.

This talk is not independent of the present debate about such schools: Should children be provided with state-funded vouchers to attend them? Should parents be given tax breaks (or should they be called incentives?) to send their children to them? Should public schools be places where such stories are told?

Yet, while the talk is not independent of this context, I want to remove my remarks as much as possible from the present debate. The debate, as important as it is, needs to be informed by a closer look at real storytelling in real schools. Here I am interested in what they can do, in what different functions they might serve, and less in what they actually do in any specific case. Once we know more about the work of such stories and the places in which they are presently told, then we will likely be able to assess better, just where, when, and how they should be told, and who should finance their telling, but these are not the topics of this essay.

Given the present debates in education it is important to look at religious stories, and to see just what they do. It is the thesis of this paper that they do not all do the same thing, and that those who speak of a religious foundation for moral education would better speak about religious foundations for different kinds of moral education, for both the religion and moral need to be understood in the plural. Thus, part of my task here is to take the very familiar and enable us to see it anew as objects of education.

The time and the place in which these stories are told – in this case twentieth-century American religious schools – is significant. The telling and the place legitimize the stories. They are not just stories; they are, for many, the most important stories. They are our stories; they are what make us the people that we are.

Different people have different stories. The place is also important because some of these stories are not everyone's stories. They are *our* stories and not their stories, and in this plurality of stories, some shared, some rejected, lies a deep conflict in American education. Are these stories sufficiently ours that we can allow them as a part of a state-supported system of schools, or, are they so different that they must forever remain separate, to be neither legitimized nor delegitimized by the state. For this talk I leave this issue for others to decide. Here I just want to look at the stories and their possible functions.

6.2   Religious Stories

Whether or not a story is religious in a certain sense depends in part upon the setting in which it is told. A story may have a religious origin, but if told in a certain setting – say a commercial movie theater, it may not be religious in the sense in which I am using the term. In order for a story with religious origins – say, "the Greatest Story Ever Told" – to be religious it needs to be told in a setting in which it is expected that it will evoke a religious attitude or produce a religious bent of mind. Religious stories, told in religious schools qualify because they have a place in the formative process of the child and are intended to infuse the child's feelings and emotions – soul if you will – with a religious bent.

Thus I begin with a seemingly simple question: What is a religious school and how does it differ from other private schools and from public ones? The answer to the question changes from time to time. Fifty years ago, a religious school would have been one that begins each day with a prayer, but then too this would have been the same for many public schools. Fifty years ago, a Catholic religious school would have been one where about 90% of the teachers were nuns. Today, however, it is only 10%. Fifty years ago, children in parochial schools would have been uniformly and categorically taught about the evils of divorce, and children would have been taught that hell as a place of fire and pain is reserved for those who sever their sacred marriage vows. Today many parochial schools must cater to children from divorced homes, and hell, when it is discussed at all, is often pictured not as a place of intense suffering and pain, but as a self-chosen removal from God.

Despite these changes a popular image persists that Catholic schools are all essentially the same, an image that no doubt reaches back to the time when the teachers were nuns, when they went from convent to school and back to convent. It was a time when the only message teachers heard was filtered through the Church hierarchy and when the only words they taught were hierarchically sanctioned. It was a time when the Baltimore catechism held sway and memory and recitation were the main pedagogical techniques.

Today, while there are still similarities from school to school, there are differences as well. You will still find crucifixes in all Catholic schools, but in some the crucifix might be embroidered on a Mexican weave, while in another, it might depict a darker, somewhat African Jesus. The catechism is still taught, but it is, despite protestations to the contrary, not your grandfather's catechism. It is newer, cooler, kinder, and it is used as a tool by teachers, and textbook writers, not as questions and answers to be committed to memory. Most of the nuns and priests are gone and in their place are lay teachers, mostly, but not all, Catholic, who travel from a home to school and back to home. And in their home, most use some form of contraception, some have been divorced, and in both home and school they may very likely confront sexually active students or gay teenagers.

There are still the same stories, but the stories may be spun in radically new directions. "Let's take Cain and Able," one Priest tells his senior class in a poor, Mexican-American school where children are brought up in broken families and where machismo is the law on the street and in the home. "Do you think they ever existed?" he asks, and quickly answering his own question, responds, "probably not, but they can serve as a symbol of a dysfunctional family." And then the discussion turns to sibling relations and jealousy. Here the story is a place to hang his hat, and to help students reflect on their own place, on their homes, as sisters and brothers, sons and daughters. About Cain and Able, the message echoes a song sung in my favorite politically incorrect musical – "It ain't necessarily so."

6.3   Differences and Similarities

In many respects, Catholic schools, at least in the United States, are not that different from public ones. There are social class differences among the schools. There are some highly regarded academic ones, much like magnet schools in the public realm where students must pass a stringent test to get into them; and there are others, often in the inner city, where the population is poor, and where completing high school is a big success. Catholic schools, like many public schools, are often financially strapped, and in many large cities the hierarchy is closing dozens of schools.

The schools that I have been engaged with are recognizably American. In the same corridors where the crucifix hangs will be the photograph of Martin Luther King, and, in the inner city, a poster warning against drugs. Counselors are confronted with pregnant girls, gay and lesbian students, alcohol and drug abuse, dysfunctional families, and divorce. Despite the fact that many American religious schools have begun to look more like American public schools, there are still important differences, and in the remainder of this chapter, I want to focus on one of the more obvious ones – the use of religious stories as tools for moral education.

Let me begin by conjuring up an image in your mind, actually two images, and let these images carry us through the inquiry. An event occurs in two different schools – a bigger child intentionally pushes a smaller one. The first is a public school and the teacher reprimands the child by asking: "How would you feel if

I pushed you?" The second is a Christian school and the teacher reprimands by asking: "How would Jesus feel about that?" In both cases imagine that the injunction is successful and the behavior is stopped. Do the words we speak make a difference, and what difference do they make?

6.4   Function of Religious Stories

Those who believe religion to be critical to moral development often assume that moral development is but one thing and that religion is the best way to achieve it. Yet religious stories serve different functions and it is more likely that each of these carries with it a somewhat different conception of morality. In other words, the moral fabric that we call religious is not obviously all of a piece, and here I want to suggest some of the different ways in which religion and morality are connected.

I focus on three functions, which I call consolidation, expansion, and constitution. Granted, however, there are other ways to analyze these stories. They comfort us in times of grief and pain, they motivate us in times of hesitation, and they inspire us when we begin to doubt our own capacity. I choose these three because they are closely related to the different ways in which we think of moral development and the ways in which children become moral agents.

First, religious stories consolidate a people, shaping their identity as this people and not that. It is the wicked son in the Passover service who asks: "[W]hy did God bring *you* out of the land of Egypt?" And the answer begins: "God brought *us* but not *you* out of the Land of Egypt because …" It is unlikely that any small child who ever listened to the story thought – I want to be left behind. In her imagination as she runs to catch up, so too does she run to join the group.

It not the question itself that makes the son wicked, but its grammar – the use of the second person and not the first person plural. Stories and the way they are told, the grammar that is used in telling them, the intimacy of the setting in which they are told, and the fact that they are told again and again from generation to generation bring us together establishing a common standpoint, stamping a shared identity and, often, a common loyalty.

I tell the same stories to my grandchildren as my grandfather told to me and in doing so I cement a bond across generations. I can recognize you as a part of me because I know that you have listened to and told the same stories that I have listened to and told. Consolidation requires special kinds of stories. They must be the story of some, but not all. In order for us to be liberated, we must first be enslaved, and there must be slave owners as well as slaves, Egyptians as well as Jews, outsiders as well as insiders. This is why many religions contain stories of us as victims – Jews persecuted by Christians, Christians persecuted by Romans, Moslems persecuted by Hindus, and in turn, Hindus by Moslems. Stories of consolidation are often stories of victimhood, of suffering, and of suffering overcome. These stories are often of heroic and epic proportion. They provide us with our heroes and our villains.

Then there are stories of extension that expand our identity into a larger, world-lier community. In practice, extension stories can work in different ways having both imperial as well as ecumenical force. Either everyone should be like us and we do them a favor when we convert them, or we are, in reality, like everyone, and need to find room for different ways of expressing devotion.

Finally, there are stories that reconstitute our moral identity in a specifically religious way and redefine what it means to be a moral person. These stories are the most difficult to describe because they share their narrative space with both stories of consolidation and extension, and thus need to be inspected for their contribution to multiple ends. Of course stories have other functions as well and these three are not exhaustive. Stories entertain, comfort, inspire, but I will leave these for another time, and simply focus on the three – consolidation, extension, and constitution – as ways in which to look at religious stories and the way in which they relate to moral education.

Let us begin with two preliminary definitions that, unsatisfactory as they are, will help to move us along. Let us define religious instruction as any form of teaching that transmits officially sanctioned understanding, practices, and beliefs of a religious order with the intent that the student should come to embrace those teachings from the inside. From the inside I mean three things: (1) that the child comes to believe them as expressing an important truth, (2) that she identifies with others who believe her, and (3) that she believes that others who believe them also identify with her.

By saying that practices and beliefs are sanctioned by the religious order, I mean that a faith community provides encouragement for holding the beliefs, for expressing them publicly, and for witnessing their expression. In this way a communal identity is sanctioned through the active encouragement of public expression. There are exceptions to this. The most famous is Jesus' Sermon on the Mount where he tells his followers to pray alone. The exception speaks about the attitude of prayer, however, and not about the formation of a religion around Jesus' teachings. In organized religions prayer serves as both worship and consolidation.

Given this definition, it is possible that a school financed and run by a religious order would not be a religious school. Say Quakers set up a school in the inner city to teach basic skills, but teach nothing about the Quaker religion and hold no religious services. The school should be classified as private with a religious affiliation, but not as a religious school as I understand the term.

Teaching students how to pray is an act of religious instruction and has a two-fold purpose – to shape the act of worship and an awareness of the spiritual and to solidify a religious identity of a certain kind. In this latter sense, it has the same function as in, say, having a child recite, with the intent of having her or him accept the definition of sin provided by the Catholic Church.

This should be contrasted with teaching students how Catholics or Hopi Indians pray, without any intent that these children should pray like Catholics or Hopis. This is not an act of religious instruction. It is instruction about religious practices. Teaching students how to meditate as a means of relaxation and where meditation is not overtly being connected to a belief system is not religious teaching. It is instruction in comparative religion where there is the aim of informing but not converting or reinforcing. Sometimes this distinction will be context-dependent. To have students reconstruct a certain religious ceremony may in some circumstances be an act of religious engagement while in others it may not be. A Moslem child who lives in a Catholic country where children are required to take part in a Catholic Mass each week is participating, willfully or not, in a religious service. However, a Catholic child who is required to recite an Islamic prayer as part of a course in comparative religion is not participating in a religious service. While there may be legitimate reasons to excuse both children from the required activity, the activities are not the same. The first is framed with the message: "This is serious. This is the way we worship God *here*." The second carries the frame: "This is an instructional exercise. See how *they* worship God."

As with any definition these have their problems, and borderline cases present difficulties. Is instruction in Zen meditation religious instruction? Possibly, but one may learn the technique without adopting many of the beliefs that go with it. Is secular humanism, with its embrace of the beliefs of science, a religious teaching? I would argue not, because it does not have a concept of the sacred, and would allow public evidence to contradict any particular belief that its members hold. It also does not have the institutional weight, the churches, priests, etc., that we associate with a religion. It might, however, be argued that it is a creed because it does accept the view that only science produces reliable knowledge, or even an ideology, although I think such arguments are weak. However, this is a side issue at this point.

To complete the exercise in definitions, I take moral instruction to be instruction aimed at advancing that which is good in the way of action and commitment. Granted, this definition, borrowed a bit from James on truth, is empty, remaining to be filled by whatever our religious instructor chooses to fill it with. Yet these definitions, as broad as they are, will be sufficient to move us along and to inquire into the question: Just what is the perceived relationship between religious instruction and moral education and how does such perception carry over into classroom work? Now let us look at the different kinds of stories and their relation to moral development.

6.5 Consolidation Stories and the Morality Connected to Them

Religion is, among other things, about miracles, revelation, and salvation. It is about how God revealed himself to Moses and then chose the Israelites for his people. It is about how "He" revealed "Himself" again through Jesus and about the miracle that Jesus performed, and the way in which the message of Jesus offers salvation; it is about how God, through the hand of an illiterate warlord, delivered, through His "last and greatest" prophet, His most complete message to His people.

Miracles are a sign of specialness. In a miracle we are saved, but we are saved not just for ourselves as individuals. Miracles assign us a purpose and that purpose makes us special. However, when I speak of consolidation, I mean something more than this. I mean a certain level of exclusiveness where the belief in a certain story and acceptance of a certain kind of evidence identifies people as belonging together. Stories may have the same quality of exclusiveness as a certain religious diet or religious circumcision. A difficult diet, an unpleasant ritual, or an implausible belief cements a bond, compels recognition, distinguishes the pure and the impure, the saved and the not saved, the insider and the outsider.

Given the role of religion in consolidating a collective identity, religious instruction is foundational to moral education because morality and its justification are traditionally bound. This connection develops out of two features of all religions. First, they depend upon the excess meaning entailed in basic life experiences. Life and death are matters of fact – we are born, we live, we die. But why we are born, why we live, and why we must die and whether asking for reasons make any sense are matters of meaning, and there are many different stories that can be told in our attempt to provide answers that will satisfy and give comfort. Second, religious beliefs bind people together into lived communities that persist across generations, and lived communities are finite and require markers with which to distinguish them from other lived communities. Belief systems much like religious symbols and rituals serve as such markers.

Because religion in the form of a community depends upon its distinctness from other communities, it is important that the core belief be of a certain kind. Beliefs that are falsifiable provide a very fragile foundation upon which to construct a religious superstructure. In this sense, the truths of religion are best placed beyond belief. Core religious beliefs cannot be of the kind that prayer cures all headaches, where we may find a headache that prayer does not cure. They must be more of the kind that Christ is a hundred percent human and a hundred percent divine, beliefs whose empirical content is beyond scrutiny, perhaps even vague. These beliefs can stand the test of time, because time could never develop a test adequate to the task. Religion thus embraces faith – truth beyond belief.

The need for religions to distinguish themselves as faith communities requires that the methods for supporting a belief will differ among them and that what counts as evidence will not always be the same. Kuhn (1962) made a similar observation with regard to scientific paradigm, claiming that those who advance competing paradigms carry with them their own methods of verification. While the idea of a crucial experiment in science may not be everything that it was once cracked up to be (Kuhn, 1962; Lakatos, 1970), Kuhn and others still held that eventually some kind of decisions could be made about the progressive or retrogressive nature of a research program. Does it make new predictions or is it compelled to simply show that the new predictions of others do not falsify a favored position? Religion does not usually bet its temporal life on such predictions and, given the importance of maintaining a distinct community, there is good reason for this. While one religion may claim superiority over all others, it does not propose a crucial experiment which, if its unique hypothesis is borne out, will support its claim, while if it is not, another religion may be declared the victor. The traditions may coexist, each with their own stories to tell, and with their own idea of truth and evidence, they may struggle against one another serving as they do to reinforce their mutual borders.

To summarize, moral stories that function to consolidate a religious identity

1. Provide a special status to one's co-religionists. This may be represented as a special place in God's heart, a special path to salvation, or a special insight into God's will.
2. Evidence for this special status will have a special status itself and understanding that evidence is one essential sign of belonging. Moslems take the Koran to be the final word of God, and the Christian and Jewish Bibles as incomplete expressions of that same word while Christians and Jews see the Koran as superfluous. Christians have the Gospel, which they hold completes the Torah, which, in turn the Jews see as superfluous. That outsiders do not accept the same evidence in the same way is a part of what makes them outsiders.
3. There is an essential division that may be expressed in terms such as the saved and the unsaved, the pure and the impure, the enlightened and the unenlightened, that sets the moral task – remain pure, separate from the unsaved, convert the unsaved, etc.
4. The moral task is often, although not always, associated with a physical place and with a return to origins – next year in Jerusalem, a pilgrimage to Mecca, an audience with the pope in Rome.

There is a meta-view, which is a philosophy about the nature of morality, that is attached to this position and it is worth mentioning here for later analysis. It holds:

- Morality is tradition bound. Without tradition there is no conception of morality.
- There is no single faculty for distinguishing good from bad. Neither moral intuition nor moral reason exists independently of a tradition.
- Moral reason and moral intuition, much like scientific reasoning and scientific logic in a Kuhnian world, are constituted through different religious paradigms.
- Traditions that are inadequate may ultimately fall apart by the weight of their own logic.
- The foundation of moral education is the teaching of a religious tradition.
- Religious traditions can be expected to have different moral codes and different modes of justification.
- Evidence is tradition-bound.
- There are no moral codes, no modes of justification, and no conception of evidence outside of a tradition.
- Since there are many traditions there are many such codes. Some overlap here or there, but each tradition and the morality it supports has its own distinct character.
- Morality across traditions may be possible because, while traditions are bounded, they are relatively so, and opportunities do appear for moral discourse about specific issues.[2]

Let me turn now to extension stories – to stories that expand our moral horizons extending them to members of other groups.

---

[2] This set of beliefs is expressed by Macintyre in *Whose Justice?*

6.6   Stories that Extend Identity

Consider the story of the Good Samaritan, a story told in response to the question "who is my neighbor?" asked in clarification of the command "You shall love your neighbor as yourself" (NAS Mark 12: 13).

The parable, told by Jesus to a Jewish scholar, goes like this: A Jew goes on a trip to Jericho and is attacked by bandits who leave him for dead. A Jewish priest comes along but crosses to the other side of the road in order to avoid him. Then another Jew comes by, looks and walks away. Finally a despised Samaritan comes along, and feeling deep pity, soothes the man's wounds and pays for a room at a local inn. Then Jesus asks: "Now which of these three would you say was a neighbor to the victim?" and the Jewish scholar replies, the man who showed him pity (TLB, Luke 10:25–37).

Note that Jesus did not say that the Samaritan was waiting on the road to help victims of bandits. Nor did the Samaritan come across the bandits in the act of theft and attempted murder, and risk his own life to save that of the victim. Rather than produce a story of a moral hero, Jesus chose something more mundane – an everyday act of kindness extended to a person, not because he was a tribal kinsman, but because he was a suffering human being. The act, while perhaps not just ordinary – Samaritans and Jews did not make it a habit of comforting, nursing, and supporting one another – was not heroic either. The parable suggests that one could meet Jesus' ideal without standing on guard, waiting with anticipation to commit a morally praiseworthy act, and it could be met without risk to one's own life.

The act has the following characteristics:

- It is an act performed with the benefit of the other foremost in mind.
- It is not an act that is required or ordered.
- It may require one to forgo an immediate desire or impulse.
- However, there will be no external punishment if the act is not performed.
- The act is performed without the expectation of a reward, although a reward might be given as an indirect consequence of the performance. Anything less would be bribery.
- The act need not be one of heroic dimension where one's own life is at risk, although moral heroism is certainly not explicitly discouraged.

In other words, it is an act that conceivably anyone could perform, and that has the intended effect of extending self-regarding feelings to others.

Now this function may be served in different ways. It may, for example, center moral behavior on one's own group while allowing that members of other groups may be included in the moral community, although sometimes unbeknownst to them. Or, it may honor the others as a moral tradition on a par with one's own and thus deserving of the same care and consideration. Some religions with an ecumenical impulse but for whom salvation is the ultimate reward must come to terms with a God who reserves salvation to right-believers, just like themselves. Catholics now allow for the unknown Christian – unknown both to themselves as well as others – to receive salvation. The problem itself represents the pull of having a good thing and wanting others to share it and the push of needing to be special and not to have that good diluted by other goods.[3]

6.7   Constitution

Consolidation and extension are functions that are not especially unique to religion. They describe much of group behavior and may be applied to tribes or to nations as well as to religions – although it is often difficult to separate the elements that bring about religious identity from those that establish a tribal or national one. The third way of thinking about religious stories cannot be separated as easily from its religious quality. It speaks to the quality of belief as well as to its content and function. To say that religious stories constitute a morality is to say that they create something that is in fact different from stories that are not religious and I want to conclude by trying to understand what this might be. I want to use the story of the Garden of Eden and the idea of original sin to illustrate this constitutive function of religion.

Take, for example, the view that some Christian theologians hold that a belief in original sin tempers the destructive features of utopian thinking. In this view, original sin is not the cause of eternal damnation; it does not serve to frighten people to believe that Christ is their only chance for salvation, or that without him they are destined to burn in the fires of hell forever and ever.

Instead, the idea of original sin, whether viewed historically or not, is taken as a metaphor that speaks of the need for humility, a need that expresses our limits as human beings, or, in theological terms, our finitude. Humility is a religious virtue because, in expressing the inherent limitations of our knowledge and our power, it expresses a fundamental fact of existence. Consider the following passage from an article by the Christian theologian Antoine Vergote:

> Belief in human perfectibility is both a necessary goal to achieve an ever-greater degree of humanity, and an insidious danger. When morality separates from its religious ground and retains the ideal of perfection, that ideal is projected on an historical future defined by reason. If there is nothing beyond human history the ideal of perfectibility has to be sought with the aid of earthly coordinates. Two dangerous possibilities are then possible. Because it realizes the actual imperfect state of things, the will to change is grossly dissatisfied. Tradition is criticized and cast aside, and so is any form of authority, for both are seen as responsible for the lack of happiness and harmony. The dream of perpetual revolution is kept alive, even though no one knows where to go despite the firm desire first to erase the traditional system in the vague belief that a new mankind will arise from the ashes as if from some aboriginal combustion. …
>
> The ideology of a perfect mankind … necessarily changes society into a Gulag. (Vergote, 1978, pp. 8–9)

---

[3] The Story of the Good Samaritan actually has this double edge to it for from the point of view of a modern Jew who reads the story as one about the moral lack of the Jewish religion when compared to that of the Christian; the story carries an Imperial tone that has a function of setting the terms for "reconciliation."

Vergote allows for the obvious objection, that the church has been tempted by the idea of perfection, although he mentions only contemporary sects. In addition to these one could add the crimes of mainstream religions – crusades, inquisitions, and religious wars. The point here, however, is not whether religion works to achieve a virtuous end, but whether it defines for us a unique virtue – whether through religion we might glimpse a stance toward virtue that would be otherwise hidden. Vergote provides some sense of what such a glimpse might be:

> In faith we know that destiny will be a glorious transformation which will complete the perfectibility of man. We know too that the historical effort made by mankind is not in vein: faith is a "power". But in confirmed ignorance about perfect humanity, and powerlessness to establish ideal humanity, and trusting in the promise, man relaxes his "tension", surrenders his exaggerated will to do good, and rejoices at the actual spark of peace, love and well-being that he is able to coax into being. . . . The symbolic power that hope imparts to the world of men frees it from that destructive violence born of a desire to being about the heavenly Jerusalem here on earth. (Ibid., p. 9)

Many will doubt that Vergote's claims to greater virtue necessarily hold for organized religion given the various crusades, jihads, and pogroms, and given the ethnic-cleansing and genocide that God seems to approve of in Samuel I. Vergote himself allows that religion can be very dangerous.

Yet there is more than just a historical claim being made here. There is a claim about the uniqueness of religious value, a uniqueness that organized religions may themselves not always live up to. Vergote emphasizes the uniqueness of the value of forgiveness and love. He notes that love your enemies is the hardest of all the commandments and the most specifically Christian one.

> True forgiveness is the real essence and means of love. Forgiveness refuses to judge and represents an act of confidence in the secret possibilities of the other's goodness. ... Forgiveness or love of one's enemies implies a refusal of any intention to identify the other with evil. . . . Forgiveness is possible only if man includes in his attitude to his enemy the attitude of the Father who, with infinite discretion, goes out to the prodigal son in order to welcome his return with joy. (Ibid., pp. 10–11)

Christian love is somewhat more controversial than Vergote might think. Many non-Christians fear that such love will provide an excuse to treat them as merely a means to their own salvation – to paraphrase Kant. Even the act of forgiveness can be taken as a power play, placing the forgiver in the position to define an act as a transgression, and granting to herself or himself the *right* to forgive. Moreover, from the Freudian perspective such love may be seen as an act of sublimation that counteracts productive attempts to deal with anger. And, the fact that Vergote writes exclusively in this essay in terms of the Father and the Son might suggest that religious virtues are largely a masculine affair.

Nevertheless, I think that there is more to Vergote's notion of religious virtue than these criticisms can fully capture. The word "love" may be too ambiguous to fully capture the idea that he has in mind. Nevertheless, the concept of love expressed here is one coupled with awe and gratitude, feelings that in turn provide a special quality to the love of attraction, compassion, and affection. It is a profound sense of gratitude for one's own being and toward being in general that I suspect informs all religion and not just Christianity. I also suspect that it is out of this sense that any uniquely religious virtue might develop. It is what is captured by a notion of religious humility.

People who have survived a catastrophe in which many others have died perhaps express this view most dramatically when they cry out "it was a miracle," or it was "God's will." To the outsider, especially the nonreligious outsider, these remarks seem self-centered. "Some miracle," we might say, "God let a thousand people die, but saved you! What did God think was so special about you?"

Yet taken generously – and of course that is what we should do given a catastrophic ordeal – these words communicate the sense that "my survival was *not* my own doing." Taken on a religious plane this kind of humility expresses a profound truth. We are all dependent on a seemingly incomprehensible set of circumstances – from the mixture of gases in the air that we breath to the distance of our planet from the sun to the speed of one particular sperm that reaches one particular egg, to all of the very unique experiences that make our life the particular life that it is.

Humility is, of course, not just a religious virtue. People can be humble for many reasons – out of respect for others, because they truly underestimate themselves, because they hate bragging whether done by others or by themselves. Or, like Burke, because they believe that human ideals can overrun human reason. Religious humility, however, is informed by the awareness of my utter dependence on the unlikely circumstances that result in my being the person who I am. It is the virtue that literally keeps us in our place as a sign that we are aware that our fate, our very being let alone our joys and our suffering, are contingent events. That all could have been otherwise.

If something like my treatment of humility does capture the religious attitude, there may well be a unique twist that religion provides to moral virtue and eventually to moral action itself. Here the morality of the act may direct us not to the belief itself, nor to its function of solidifying or extending an identity, important as these are, but in the way a belief is held, recognizing that contingency of being may well extend to contingency of believing and that religious humility promotes not only recognition that we all labor under the possibility of error, that forgiveness is an imperative because of ontological uncertainty about who deserves to occupy the role of forgiver.

6.8   Conclusion: What Would Jesus Want?

I want to conclude by returning to the educational side of the equation, and to the question that what difference does it make if the teacher asks: "How would you feel if I pushed you?" Or if she asks: "What would Jesus want?" I have suggested one answer to this question. Asking what Jesus wants is not simply addressing a slice of behavior, but it involves as well an induction into a moral community with certain beliefs and practices that distinguish it from other moral communities. Whether the message is used to extend as well as to consolidate, and if used to extend, whether it will entail a hegemonic or an ecumenical extension depends on how other instructional messages are delivered.

Yet there is a potentially problematic side of wanting to please Jesus that educators must be concerned about and I want to conclude with some remarks about this. Young children learn moral behavior, as both Aristotle and James understood, by first acting and then developing dispositions to act in a certain way given a certain kind of situation. In developing such dispositions, there are many legitimate motivators and some illegitimate ones. Pleasing someone close to you is certainly a feature of moral motivation in young children, and later a more abstract, if in some cases, no less intimate figure, like thinking from the point of view of Jesus or of justice or mercy, may well take over. However, early motivators can be problematic. If they connect too quickly to a behavior, thought could be short-circuited and reasoning curtailed. Thus it is important not to confuse religious instruction which may well contribute to moral education with moral education itself. To illustrate this, let us take a simple act of learning to please Jesus and what that learning entails. Take as an example the brief list that I gave earlier as marking the minimal conditions for pleasing Jesus:

1. It is an act performed with the benefit of the other foremost in mind.
2. It is not an act that is required or ordered.
3. It may require one to forgo an immediate desire or impulse.
4. There will be no external punishment if the act is not performed.
5. The act is performed without the expectation of a reward, although a reward might be given as an indirect consequence of the performance. Anything less would be bribery.
6. The act need not be one of heroic dimension where one's own life is at risk, although moral heroism is certainly not to be discouraged.

I have left out of the list that the act must please Jesus. There are three reasons for this omission: a religious one, a scientific one, and an educational one. The religious reason is rather simple; namely, the relationship between actor and Jesus is personal, and has an ultimately private dimension to it. Ultimately only Jesus and the agent can know what is "in the heart" of the actor. The other two reasons are a bit more complex.

The scientific reason is that the dimensions of the act must be open to inspection and others must be able to tell whether it meets the criteria. The six items allow for a public appraisal. Pleasing Jesus does not. Granted, we may argue about the private or public status of intentions. My own view is that intentions need not be exclusively private although like many things that have a public status they can be hidden from view. However, it is difficult to claim that a person's relationship to Jesus is public in the same way. This is different from the judgment about a person's sincerity. One could sincerely believe that she has pleased Jesus and be mistaken. And, another person may more accurately assess whether the person sincerely believes that she has pleased Jesus. What they cannot assess is whether, in the usual sense of the term, Jesus is pleased.

Operationally then the six criteria stipulate what it means to perform an act that could be said to please Jesus. If Jesus had a checklist of items that needed to be met in order for him to be pleased, this is the list he would consult. He would consult each item, check them off, and then, when all have been satisfied, he would produce a sign of pleasure, or say something like "I am *really* pleased."[4]

The educational reason for not including "pleasing Jesus" is the most important one for this discussion. A person in need of "education" implies a gap between the person as actor and the person as knower, or as agent of the act – a gap that arises out of a certain implied ignorance on the part of the actor about the connection between the act and the reasons for the act. Agency implies responsibility, and responsibility implies an understanding of the relation between act and consequences. Education takes place to inform the actor about that relation. The process of education involves developing the ability to judge the merits of reasons and the autonomy to act on them.

Hence a child may perform an act that essentially meets the criteria and be told by her parents that Jesus is pleased, but not have the ability to understand how the act might please Jesus. Take a three-year-old who places a quarter in the collection box. She puts a quarter in the box believing that doing so will please Jesus. However, she does not yet understand what a quarter is, or *that* it can be, used to buy food for a hungry child. The act then meets the criteria, but because the connection between placing the quarter in the box, and providing food for the hungry is not yet available to her, Jesus would not be pleased, but then again he would not be displeased either. Is this perhaps what traditional Church meant by limbo?

Thus a child may perform an act that essentially meets the criteria and be told by her parents that Jesus is pleased, and thus join her pleasure to that of Jesus (which is presumably the intent of the statement) but not have the ability to understand how the act might please Jesus.

The point is that moral education requires an understanding not just of the consequences of the act, but of the reasons why some consequences are more likely to occur than others. In other words, it requires in part an empirical frame of mind, and the capacity to assess the merits of the reasons that are given to us. To want to please Jesus, Allah, or Yahweh may well serve as a moral exemplar, providing the initial motive, but the motive will not be complete until there is a willingness to take a hard look at the effects of an act and the source of a belief. To this end moral education within a religious context would include a fair appraisal of the conflicts that arise within the religious community and the arguments advanced on different sides.

---

[4] There is one theological question that I need to raise but am in no position to answer. It is possible that an act could be performed that meets all six criteria without the actor having any knowledge of Jesus, or without intending to please Jesus. Will the act still please Jesus or must the actor actually intend to please Jesus in order for it to do so. I do not know the answer to this question, but while it is important for the question of salvation – can a good person who never heard of Jesus be saved, it does not related to the question at hand – what does it take to please Jesus? All that needs to be said is that it is possible that the six criteria may be necessary, but may not be sufficient.

Yet if my argument is correct, it also may suggest a more humble attitude from religious educators themselves when counseling children and adults about moral behavior. An attitude of humility toward the universe does not tell us what is right or wrong in any particular circumstances. It may tell us that we are not completely alone, and that we would do well when confronted with a moral issue to look at the wisdom of others as we decide what action to take. It may also allow that pedagogically students need moral guidance and at least provisional rules about the good and the right. It may even allow that we cannot fully reason with children and that we need to develop trusting relationships with them as we develop and expand their capacity to reason for themselves. Yet the same humility that speaks to the need for adult guidance may also require moral and religious leaders to be more circumspect about micro-managing moral behavior with a set of rules that curtail the creative expression of others. This, however, is an issue for another time.

References

Kuhn, T. (1962). *The structure of scientific revolutions*. Chicago, IA: University of Chicago Press.

Lakatos, I. (1970). Falsification and the methodology of scientific research programmes. In I. Lakatos and A. Musgrave (Eds.), *Criticism and the growth of knowledge* (pp. 91–197). Cambridge: Cambridge University Press.

MacIntyre, A. (1988). *Whose justice, which rationality?*. Notre Dame, IA: University of Notre Dame Press.

Vergote, A. (1978). God our Father. In Böckle, F and Pohier, J.M (Eds.), *Moral formation and Christianity*. New York: The Seabury Press.

Chapter 7
Sporadic Democracy: Education, Democracy, and the Question of Inclusion

Gert Biesta

Abstract In this chapter I take up the question of the relationship between democracy and inclusion. I present the deliberative turn in democratic theory as an attempt to overcome "external exclusion" and discuss Iris Young's work as an attempt to overcome "internal exclusions". I argue that although attempts to make democracy more inclusive are laudable, they are ultimately based upon a colonial conception of democratisation, one in which inclusion is seen as a process where those who are already on the inside include others into their sphere. I use the work of Jacques Rancière to argue for an understanding of democratisation as the interruption of the existing political order from the outside in the name of equality. This can not only help us to think differently about the role of inclusion in democracy, it also urges us to see that there are opportunities for the democratisation of education that lie beyond the inclusion of "newcomers" into the existing democratic order.

> The guarantee of democracy is not the filling up of all the dead times and empty spaces by the forms of participation or of counterpower: it is the continual renewal of the actors and of the forms of their actions, the ever-open possibility of the fresh emergence of this fleeting subject.
>
> Jacques Rancière (1995, p.61)

7.1 Democracy and Inclusion

It could well be argued that inclusion is one of the core values, if not *the* core value of democracy. The "point" of democracy, after all, is the inclusion of everyone (the whole *demos*) into the ruling (*kratein*) of society. This is why Pericles defined democracy as the situation in which "power is in the hands not of a minority but of the whole people" (Held, 1987, p.16), and also why Aristotle wrote about democracy as the "rule of all over each and of each by turns over all" (ibid., p.19). Inclusion

Gert Biesta
Institute of Education, University of Stirling
Scotland, UK

M.S. Katz et al. (eds.) *Education, Democracy, and the Moral Life*,
© Springer Science + Business Media, B.V. 2009

also affects the legitimacy of democracy because, as Iris Young has pointed out, the normative legitimacy of democratic decision-making precisely depends "on the degree to which those affected by it have been included in the decision-making processes and have had the opportunity to influence the outcomes" (Young, 2000, pp.5–6).

Inclusion is not only the main point and purpose of democracy, it is also one of its main problems. The question that has haunted democracy from day one (and in a sense already troubled democracy before it took off) is the question "Who are to be included in the [definition of the] *demos*?" This is the question of *democratic citizenship* and we know all too well that in the city state of Athens citizenship was a highly restricted affair. Only Athenian men over the age of 20 were eligible for citizenship. Women, children, slaves (who made up about 60% of the population) and immigrants, even from families who had settled in Athens several generations earlier, were simply excluded from political participation (Held, 1987, p.23).

On the one hand the history of democracy can be written as a continuous quest for inclusion. Some of the most powerful and successful social movements of the last century – including the women's movement and the labour movement – have precisely mobilised "around demands for oppressed and marginalized people to be included as full and equal citizens" (Young, 2000, p.6). But the history of democracy is at the very same time a history of *exclusion*. In some cases exclusion is justified in the name of democracy. This is, for example, the case with *liberal* democracy where the democratic principle of popular rule (expressing the principle of *equality*) is qualified by a set of basic liberties that take priority over popular rule in order to make sure that popular rule does not restrain or obstruct individual freedom (thus expressing the principle of *liberty*) (Gutmann, 1993, p.413). Whereas liberal democracy seeks to exclude certain *outcomes* of democratic decision-making (and thus would exclude those who would argue for such outcomes), there is also a more direct link between democracy and exclusion. The overriding argument here focuses on those who are deemed not to be "fit" for democracy, either because they lack certain qualities that are considered to be fundamental for democratic participation – such as rationality or reasonableness (see below) – or because they do not subscribe to the ideal of democracy itself.

As Bonnie Honig (1993) has argued, this is not only an issue for communitarians who wish to see democratic politics organised around particular political identities. It is also an issue for liberals since they tend to restrict political participation to those who are willing and able to act in a rational way and who are willing to leave their substantive conceptions of the good life behind them in the private sphere. Such strategies not only result in the exclusion of those who are considered to be "sub-rational" (e.g. certain categories of psychiatric patients) or unreasonable. They are also used to justify the exclusion of those who we might call "pre-rational" or, in a more general sense, "pre-democratic", and children are the most obvious example of such a category. It is here, then, that there is an important link with education, because democratic education is often seen as the process that should make individuals "ready" for their participation in democratic decision-making (for a critical discussion of this view of democratic education see Biesta & Lawy, 2006; Biesta, 2006, 2007).

In this chapter I ask what it means for democracy to be inclusive and I discuss how democracy might become more inclusive – although I will argue that, in a sense, this is the wrong question. I start with an overview of recent developments in democratic theory, focusing on the deliberative turn (Dryzek) and the work of Iris Young. I argue that although these developments have the potential to make democratic deliberation and decision-making more inclusive, they rely on a set of assumptions, which, from the point of view of inclusion, are problematic. I then turn to the work of Jacques Rancière to explore a different way to understand the relationship between inclusion and democracy. In the concluding section I argue why Rancière's approach is important, both for our understanding of democracy and of democratic education.

7.2   The Role of Inclusion in Democratic Theory

The question of inclusion plays a central role in discussions about political decision-making. In contemporary political theory there are two main models of democratic decision-making: the *aggregative* model and the *deliberative* model (see Young, 2000, pp.18–26; Elster, 1998, p.6). The first model sees democracy as a process of aggregating the preferences of individuals, often, but not exclusively, in choosing public officials and policies. A central assumption is that the preferences of individuals should be seen as given and that politics is only concerned with the aggregation of preferences, often, but not exclusively, on the basis of majority rule. Where these preferences come from, whether they are valid or not, and whether they are held for egoistic or altruistic reasons is considered to be irrelevant. The *aggregative* model assumes, in other words, "that ends and values are subjective, non-rational, and exogenous to the political process" and that democratic politics is basically "a competition between private interests and preferences" (Young, 2000, p.22).

Over the past two decades an increasing number of political theorists have argued that democracy should not be confined to the simple aggregation of preferences but should involve the *deliberative transformation* of preferences. Under the deliberative model democratic decision-making is seen as a process which involves "decision making by means of arguments offered *by* and *to* participants" (Elster, 1998, p.8) about the means *and* the ends of collective action. As Young explains, deliberative democracy is not about "determining what preferences have greatest numerical support, but [about] determining which proposals the collective agrees are supported by the best reasons" (Young, 2000, p.23). The reference to "best reasons" indicates – and this is very important – that deliberative democracy is based upon a particular conception of deliberation. Dryzek, for example, acknowledges that deliberation can cover a rather broad spectrum of activities but argues that for *authentic* deliberation to happen the requirement is that the reflection on preferences should take place in a *non-coercive* manner (Dryzek, 2000, p.2). This requirement, so he explains, "rules out domination via the exercise of power, manipulation, indoctrination, propaganda, deception, expression of mere self-interest, threats . . . and attempts to impose ideological conformity" (ibid.). This resonates with Elster's claim that deliberative democracy is about the giving and taking of arguments by participants "who are committed to the values of rationality and impartiality" (Elster, 1998, p.8) and with his suggestion that deliberation must take place between "free, equal and rational agents" (ibid., p.5).

In one respect the "deliberative turn" (or re-turn; see Dryzek, 2000, pp.1–2) is an important step forward in democratic theory and democratic practice. On the one hand it seems to be a more full expression of the basic values of democracy, particularly the idea that democracy is about actual participation in collective decision-making. In the aggregative model there is, after all, little participation, and decision-making is mainly algorithmic. On the other hand, the deliberative approach seems to have a much stronger educational potential. In the deliberative model "political actors not only express preferences and interest, but they *engage* with one another about how to balance these under circumstances of inclusive equality" (Young, 2000, p.26; emphasis added). Such interaction "requires participants to be open and attentive to one another, to justify their claims and proposals in terms of [being] acceptable to all, the orientation of participants moves from self-regard to an orientation to what is publicly assertable" (ibid.). Thus "people often gain new information, learn different experiences of their collective problems, or find that their own initial opinions are founded on prejudice and ignorance, or that they have misunderstood the relation of their own interests to others" (ibid.). As Warren has put it, participation in deliberation can make individuals "more public-spirited, more tolerant, more knowledgeable, more attentive to the interests of others, and more probing of their own interests" (Warren, 1992, p.8). Deliberative democracy, so its proponents argue, is therefore not only more *democratic* but also more *educative*. A third asset of deliberative democracy lies in its potential impact on the *motivation* of political actors in that participation in democratic decision-making is more likely to commit participants to its outcomes. This suggests that deliberative democracy is not only an intrinsically desirable way of social problem-solving but probably also an effective way of doing this (see Dryzek, 2000, p. 172).

The deliberative turn can be seen as an attempt to bring democracy closer to its core values and in this respect represents an important correction to the individualism and "disconnected pluralism" (Biesta, 2006) of the aggregative model and of liberal democracy more generally. However, by raising the stakes of democracy, deliberative democracy has also brought the difficulty of democratic inclusion into much sharper focus, and thus has generated – ironically but not surprisingly – a series of problems around the question of inclusion. The main issue here centres on the *entry conditions for participation* in deliberation. The authors quoted above all seem to suggest that participation in democratic deliberation should be regulated and that it should be confined to those who commit themselves to a particular set of values and behaviours. Young, for example, argues that the deliberative model "entails several normative ideas for the relationships and dispositions of deliberating parties, among them inclusion, equality, reasonableness, and publicity" which, so she claims, "are all *logically* related in the deliberative model" (Young, 2000, p.23; emphasis added). Most of the proponents of (versions of) deliberative democracy specify a set of entry conditions for participation, although what is interesting about the discussion is that most go at great pains to delineate a *minimum* set of conditions necessary for democratic deliberation rather than an ideal set (see, e.g. the contributions in Elster, 1998). Young provides an interesting example with her distinction between reasonableness (which she sees as a necessary entry condition) and rationality (which she doesn't see as a necessary condition). For Young being reasonable doesn't entail being rational. Reasonableness refers to "a set of *dispositions* that discussion participants have [rather] than to the substance of people's contributions to debate" (Young, 2000, p.24; emphasis added). She concedes that reasonable people "often have crazy ideas," yet "what makes them reasonable is their willingness to listen to others who want to explain to them why their ideas are incorrect or inappropriate" (ibid.). In Young's hands reasonableness thus emerges as a communicative *virtue*, and not as a criterion for the logical "quality" of people's preferences and convictions.

This example not only shows why the issue of inclusion is so prominent in the deliberative model. It also explains why the deliberative turn has generated a whole new set of issues around inclusion. The reason for this is that deliberation is not simply a form of political decision-making but first and foremost a form of political *communication*. The inclusion question in deliberative democracy is therefore not so much a question about who should be included – although this question should be asked always as well. It is first and foremost a question about who is able to participate effectively in deliberation. As Dryzek aptly summarises, the suspicion about deliberative democracy is "that its focus on a particular kind of reasonable political interaction is not in fact neutral, but systematically excludes a variety of voices from effective participation in democratic politics" (Dryzek, 2000, p.58). In this regard Young makes a helpful distinction between two forms of exclusion: *external exclusion*, which is about "how people are [actually] kept outside the process of discussion and decision-making", and *internal exclusion* where people are formally included in decision-making processes but where they may find, for example, "that their claims are not taken seriously and may believe that they are not treated with equal respect" (Young, 2000, p.55). Internal exclusion, in other words, refers to those situations in which people "lack effective opportunity to influence the thinking of others even when they have access to fora and procedures of decision-making" (ibid.) which can particularly be the outcome of the emphasis of some proponents of deliberative democracy on "dispassionate, unsituated, neutral reason" (ibid. p.63).

To counteract the internal exclusion that is the product of a too narrow focus on argument, Young has suggested several other modes of political communication which should be added to the deliberative process not only to remedy "exclusionary tendencies in deliberative practices" but also to promote "respect and trust" and to make possible "understanding across structural and cultural difference" (ibid. p.57). The first of these is *greeting* or *public acknowledgement*. This is about "communicative political gestures through which those who have conflicts . . . *recognize* others as included in the discussion, especially those with whom they differ in opinion, interest, or social location" (ibid., p.61; emphasis in original). Young emphasises that greeting should be thought of as a starting-point for political interaction. It "*precedes* the giving and evaluating of reasons" (ibid., p.79) and does so through the recognition of the other parties in the deliberation. The second mode of political communication is *rhetoric* and more specifically the affirmative use of rhetoric (ibid., p.63). Although one could say that rhetoric only concerns the form of political communication and not its content, the point Young makes is that inclusive political communication should pay attention to and be inclusive about the different forms of expression and should not try to purify rational argument from rhetoric. Rhetoric is not only important because it can help to get particular issues on the agenda for deliberation. Rhetoric can also help to articulate claims and arguments "*in ways appropriate to a particular public in a particular situation*" (ibid., p.67; emphasis in original). Rhetoric always accompanies an argument by situating it "for a particular audience and giving it embodied style and tone" (ibid., p.79). Young's third mode of political communication is *narrative* or *storytelling*. The main function of narrative in democratic communication lies in its potential "to foster understanding among members of a polity with very different experience or assumptions about what is important" (ibid., p.71). Young emphasises the role of narrative in the teaching and learning dimension of political communication. "Inclusive democratic communication", so she argues, "assumes that all participants have something to teach the public about the society in which they dwell together" and also assumes "that all participants are ignorant of some aspects of the social or natural world, and that everyone comes to a political conflict with some biases, prejudices, blind spots, or stereo-types" (ibid., p.77).

It is important to emphasise that greeting, rhetoric and narrative are not meant to *replace* argumentation. Young stresses again and again that deliberative democracy entails "that participants require reasons of one another and critically evaluate them" (ibid., p.79). Other proponents of the deliberative model take a much more narrow approach and see deliberation exclusively as a form of *rational* argumentation (e.g. Benhabib, 1996) where the only legitimate force should be the "forceless force of the better argument" (Habermas). Similarly, Dryzek, after a discussion of Young's ideas,[1] concludes that argument always has to be "central to deliberative democracy" (Dryzek, 2000, p.71). Although he acknowledges that other modes of communication can be present and that there are good reasons to welcome them, their status is different "because they do not *have* to be present" (ibid., emphasis added). For Dryzek, at the end of the day, all modes of political communication must live up to the standards of rationality. This does not mean that they must be

---

[1] Dryzek refers to work published by Young before her in *Inclusion and Democracy*. Several of the issues Dryzek raises about Young's position seem no longer to be part of the position she takes in *Inclusion and Democracy*.

subordinated to rational argument "but their deployment only makes sense in a context where argument about what is to be done remains central" (ibid., p.168).

7.3 Can Democracy Become "Normal"?

This brief overview of inclusion reveals the progress that has been made over the past two decades around the question of democratic inclusion. But this is not to suggest that there are no problems left with the direction in which the discussion about democratic inclusion is moving – and these problems, so I wish to suggest, are not merely practical but have to do with more fundamental assumptions that underlie the discourse about democracy and inclusion. There are two assumptions which, in my view, are particularly problematic.

One assumption is the belief that democracy can become a "normal" situation. In the discussion about inclusion the main challenge seems to be perceived as a *practical* one, i.e. as the question how we can make our democratic practices even more inclusive (internal inclusion) and how we can include even more people into the sphere of democratic deliberation (external inclusion). The assumption here is that if we can become even more attentive to otherness and difference, we will eventually reach a situation of total democratic inclusion, a situation in which democracy has become "normal". While people may have different views about when and how this situation might be reached and whether or not there will always be some "remainders" (Mouffe, 1993), the idea that democratisation means including more and more people into the sphere of democracy reveals the underlying idea that the best democracy is the most inclusive democracy, and reveals the underlying assumption that democracy can and should become a normal political reality.

This relates to a second assumption, which is the idea that inclusion should be understood as a process in which those who stand outside of the sphere of democracy should be brought into this sphere and, more importantly, should be included by those who are already on the inside. The assumption here is that inclusion is a process which happens "from the inside out", a process which emanates from the position of those who are already considered to be democratic. The very language of inclusion not only suggests that someone is including someone else, it also suggests – and this, of course, is familiar terrain for those who work in the field of inclusive education – that someone is setting the terms for inclusion and that it is for those who wish to be included to meet those terms.

There is, of course, no need to throw out the baby of deliberative democracy with the bathwater of theoretical purity, and this is definitely not my intention. Deliberative democracy clearly has many advantages over other political practices and processes. But the question we should ask is whether the underlying assumptions about democracy result in the best and, so we might say, most democratic way to understand and "do" democracy. The first step in answering this question is to ask whether democracy can be understood differently. One author who has tried to approach the question of democracy in a way that is indeed different from the prevailing discourse about democracy and inclusion is Jacques Rancière.

7.4 Rancière on Democracy and Democratisation

Whereas in the prevailing discourse democracy is seen as something that can be permanent and normal, Rancière argues for an understanding of democracy as *sporadic*, as something that only "happens" from time to time and in very particular situations (see Rancière, 1995, p.41, p.61). To clarify this point Rancière makes a distinction between politics – which for him always means *democratic* politics (democracy as "the institution of politics itself" – Rancière, 1999, p.101) – and what he refers to as *police* or *police order*. In a way that is reminiscent of Foucault, Rancière defines the police as "an order of bodies that defines the allocation of ways of doing, ways of being, and ways of saying, and that sees that those bodies are assigned by name to a particular place and task" (Rancière, 1999, p.29). It as an order "of the visible and the sayable that sees that a particular activity is visible and another is not, that this speech is understood as discourse and another as noise" (ibid.). Police should not be understood as the way in which the state structures the life of society. It is not, in Habermasian terms, the "grip" of the system on the life world, but includes *both*. As Rancière explains, "[t] he distribution of places and roles that defines a police regime stems as much from the assumed spontaneity of social relations as from the rigidity of state functions" (ibid.). One way to read this definition of police is to think of it as an order that is *all-inclusive* in that everyone has a particular place, role, or position in it. This is not to say that everyone is included in the running of the order. The point simply is that no one is excluded from the order. After all, women, children, slaves, and immigrants had a clear place in the democracy of Athens, viz., as those who were not allowed to participate in political decision-making. In precisely this respect every police order is all-inclusive.

Against this background Rancière then defines *politics* as the disruption of the police order in the name of equality. This may sound simpler than what Rancière has in mind, so it is important to be clear about the kind of disruption politics represents. Rancière explains that he reserves the term *politics* "for an extremely determined activity antagonistic to policing: whatever breaks with the tangible configuration whereby parties and parts or lack of them are defined by a presupposition that, by definition, has no place in that configuration" (ibid., pp.30–31). This break is manifest is a series of actions "that reconfigure the space where parties, parts, or lack of parts have been defined". (ibid., p.31). Political activity so conceived is "whatever shifts a body from the place assigned to it" (ibid.). "It makes visible what had no business being seen, and makes heard [and understood; G.B.] a discourse where once there was only place for noise" (ibid.).

> [P]olitical activity is always a mode of expression that undoes the perceptible divisions of the police order by implementing a basically heterogeneous assumption, that of a part of

those who have no part, an assumption that, at the end of the day, itself demonstrates the sheer contingency of the order [and] the equality of any speaking being with any other speaking being. (ibid)

Politics thus refers to the event when two "heterogeneous processes" meet: the police process and the process of *equality* (see ibid.).

There are two points to add to this account. The first is that for Rancière politics understood in this way is always *democratic* politics. Democracy, so he argues, "is not a regime or a social way of life" – it is not and cannot be, in other words, part of the police order – but should rather be understood "as the institution of politics itself" (ibid., p.101). Every politics is democratic *not* in the sense of a set of institutions, but in the sense of forms of expression "that confront the logic of equality with the logic of the police order" (ibid.). Democracy, so we might say, is a "claim" for equality.

But this raises a further question about Rancière's understanding of democracy, which is *who* it is that makes this claim. Who, in other words, "does" politics or "performs' democracy?[2] The point of asking the question in this way is not to suggest that there is no subject of politics, that there are no democratic actors involved in democracy. The point is that political actors – or subjects – do not exist *before* the "act" of democracy, or to be more precise: their political identity, their identity as democratic subjects only comes into being in and through the act of disruption of the police order. This is why Rancière argues that politics is itself a process of *subjectification*. It is a process in and through which political subjects are constituted. Rancière defines subjectification as "the production through a series of actions of a body and a capacity for enunciation not previously identifiable within a given field of experience, whose identification is thus part of the reconfiguration of the field of experience" (ibid., p.35).

Democracy – or to be more precise, the appearance of democracy – is therefore not simply the situation in which a group who has previously been excluded from the realm of politics steps forward to claim its place under the sun. It is at the very same time the *creation* of a group as group with a particular identity that did not exist before. Democratic activity is, for example, to be found in the activity of 19th-century workers "who established a collective basis for work relations" that were previously seen as "the product of an infinite number of relationships between private individuals" (ibid., p.30). Democracy thus establishes new, *political* identities. Or as Rancière puts it: "Democracy is the designation of subjects that do not coincide with the parties of the state or of society" (ibid., pp.99–100). This means that "the place where the people appear" is the place "where a dispute is conducted" (ibid., p.100). The political dispute is distinct from all conflicts of interest between constituted parties of the population, for it is a conflict "over the very count of those parties" (ibid.). It is a dispute between "the police logic of the distribution of places and the political logic of the egalitarian act" (ibid.). Politics is therefore "primarily

---

[2] I am aware that this is a rather clumsy way of putting the question, but it is consistent with Rancière's line of thinking. He himself writes at some point about '[t]he people through which democracy occurs' (Rancière, 1999, p.99).

a conflict over the existence of a common stage and over the existence and status of those present on it" (ibid., pp.26–27).

For Rancière, therefore, democratisation is *not* a process that emanates from the centre and extends to the margins. It is not a process in which those who are already democratic – an impossible position from Rancière's point of view anyway – include others into their sphere. Rather democracy appears as a claim from the "outside", a claim based upon the perception of injustice, or of what Rancière refers to as a "wrong", a claim made in the name of equality. Those who make the claim do not simply want to be included in the existing order; they want to *redefine* the order in such a way that *new* identities, new ways of doing and being become possible and can be "counted". This means that for Rancière democratisation is no longer a process of inclusion of excluded parties into the existing order; it rather is a transformation of that order in the name of equality. The impetus for this transformation does not come from the inside but rather from the outside. But it is important to see that, unlike in the prevailing discourse about democratic inclusion, this outside is not a "known" outside. Democratisation is, after all, not a process that happens *within* the police order in which it is perfectly clear who are taking part in decision-making and who are not. Democratisation is a process that *disrupts* the existing order from a place that could not be expressed or articulated from within this order.

It is, finally, important to see that for Rancière the purpose of democracy and the "point" of democratisation is not to create constant chaos and disruption. Although Rancière would maintain that democratisation is basically a good thing, this does not mean that the police order is necessarily bad. Although this may not be very prominent in Rancière's work, he does argue that democratisation can have a positive effect on the police order. Democratic disputes do produce what he refers to as "inscriptions of equality" (ibid., 100); they leave traces behind in the (transformed) police order. This is why Rancière emphasises that "[t]here is a worse and a better police" (ibid., pp.30–31). The better one is, however, not the one "that adheres to the supposedly natural order of society or the science of legislators" – it is the one "that all the breaking and entering perpetrated by egalitarian logic has most jolted out of its "natural' logic" (ibid., p.31). Rancière thus acknowledges that the police "can produce all sorts of good, and one kind of police may be infinitely preferable to another" (ibid., p.31). But, so he concludes, whether the police is "sweet and kind" does not make it any less the opposite of politics (see ibid.).

7.5 Conclusions

Is this chapter I have indicated two problems with the way in which inclusion has been thematised in recent developments in democratic theory. Both problems are related, since they both have to do with a particular understanding of the process of *democratisation*. As I have shown, democratisation is basically understood as a process through which those who are not yet part of the sphere of democracy become included in it. This, as I have argued, suggests that the envisaged end point for democracy is the situation in which *everyone* is included, the situation in which democracy has become the normal political situation. It also suggests a set up in which some are already inside the "sphere" of democracy and where it is up to them to include others into *their* practice.

I have shown that there are several problems with this understanding of democracy and democratisation. The main problem is that it is premised on the idea that we – and the key question is of course who the "we" here is – already know what democracy is and that inclusion is nothing more than bringing more people into the existing democratic order. This is basically a colonial way to understand democratisation and it is precisely the logic behind what I see as the imperialistic expansion of (a certain definition of) democracy which is currently happening at the geopolitical level. The main problem with this approach is that the political order itself, the democracy in which others are being included, is taken for granted; it is the starting point that itself cannot be questioned. This is not only a problem for international politics. It is at the same time a problem for those forms of democratic education which operate on the assumption that it is the task of democratic education to include children and other "newcomers" into the existing democratic order by facilitating a transition from a pre-rational and pre-democratic stage to a stage at which children have met the entry conditions for their future participation in democracy.

The importance of Rancière's work lies precisely in the fact that he puts this way of thinking about democracy and inclusion on its head. For him democracy is not a normal situation, i.e. it is not a way in which the police order exists, but rather occurs in the interruption of the order in the name of equality – which is why he says that democracy is sporadic. Furthermore, democratisation for Rancière is not something that is done *to* others; it is something that people can only do themselves. Rancière connects this to the question of emancipation. Emancipation, he writes, means "escaping from a minority" (Rancière, 1995, p.48). But he adds to this that "nobody escapes from the social minority save by their own efforts" (ibid.). Thirdly, Rancière helps us to see that we should understand democratic inclusion not in terms of adding more people to the existing order, but rather as a process that necessarily involves the transformation of that order. As long as we restrict our inclusive efforts to those who are known to be excluded, we only operate within the existing order. This, so I wish to emphasise, is definitely not *un*important because, as Rancière reminds us, there is a worse and a better police. But what Rancière provides us with is an understanding of the need for a different kind of inclusion: the inclusion of what cannot be known to be excluded in terms of the existing order; the inclusion of what I have elsewhere referred to as the "incalculable" (see Biesta, 2001).

Why and how do these ideas matter for education and, more importantly, for democratic education? In my view it is first of all of the utmost importance in the current political climate to have ways of thinking and "doing" democratic education that are precisely *not* informed by a colonial view of democratic education. Rancière at the very least shows us that it is possible to understand the relationship between democracy, democratisation, and inclusion differently, in a way that is far less tainted by a colonial frame of mind. Rancière also helps us to see that there is a choice. Democratic education can either play a role in the police order – and I wish to emphasise that there is important work to be done there as well – or it can try to link up with experiences and practices of democratisation that come from the "outside" and interrupt the democratic order in the name of equality. Instead of teaching children and young people to be "good democrats" – which, in my view, is a strategy that basically remains within the police order – educators may well have a role to play in utilising and supporting the learning opportunities in those incalculable moments when democratisation "occurs". That such moments might occur as the interruption of attempts to teach democracy – even if it is a teaching based on deliberative idea(l)s – is, in my view, something that goes without saying.

References

Benhabib, S. (1996). Toward a deliberative model of democratic legitimacy. In S. Benhabib (Ed.), *Democracy and difference* (pp. 67–94). Princeton, NJ: Princeton University Press.

Biesta, G. (2001). Preparing for the incalculable. Deconstruction, justice and the question of education. In G. Biesta & D. Egéa-Kuehne (Eds.), *Derrida & education* (pp. 32–54). London/New York: Routledge.

Biesta, G. (2006). *Beyond learning: Democratic education for a human future*. Boulder, CO: Paradigm.

Biesta, G., & R. Lawy (2006). From teaching citizenship to learning democracy. Overcoming individualism in research, policy and practice. *Cambridge Journal of Education*, 36, 63–79.

Biesta, G. (2007). Education and the democratic person: Towards a political understanding of democratic education. *Teachers College Record*, 109, 740–769.

Dryzek, J. (2000). *Deliberative democracy and beyond: Liberals, critics, contestations*. Oxford: Oxford University Press.

Elster, J. (Ed) (1998). *Deliberative democracy*. Cambridge: Cambridge University Press.

Gutmann, A. (1993). Democracy. In R. Goodin & P. Pettit (Eds.), *A companion to contemporary political philosophy* (pp. 411–421). Oxford: Blackwell.

Held, D. (1987). *Models of democracy*. Cambridge: Polity Press.

Honig, B. (1993). *Political theory and the displacement of politics*. Ithaca, NY: Cornell University Press.

Mouffe, C. (1993). *The return of the political*. London/New York: Verso.

Rancière, J. (1995). *On the shores of politics*. London/New York: Verso.

Rancière, J. (1999). *Dis-agreement: Politics and philosophy*. Minneapolis, MN/London: University of Minnesota Press.

Warren, M. (1992). Democratic theory and self-transformation. *American Political Science Review*, 86, 8–23.

Young, I. (2000). *Inclusion and democracy*. Oxford: Oxford University Press.

Chapter 8
Public Reason and the Education of Democratic Citizens: The Role of Higher Education[1*]

Emily Robertson

Abstract Recent public discourse in the United States has often been polarized, contentious, and filled with half-truths and misconceptions, if not outright lies. Like the Queen in *Alice in Wonderland*, some citizens seem able to believe "six impossible things before breakfast." Many colleges and universities have committed themselves to helping form socially responsible citizens as a central part of their mission, a task long embraced by public education. What are the knowledge, skills, and commitments – the citizen virtues – on which a healthy liberal democracy depends? And what role, if any, can higher education play in developing them?

8.1 The Contemporary Context for Civic Education

In the wake of the 2004 presidential election, there were numerous analyses of the quality of public political discussion. "Does the Truth Matter Anymore?" was a headline for an article on the election in my local newspaper by colleagues from Syracuse's Maxwell School of Citizenship and Public Affairs, Grant Reeher and John Mero (2004). They note that political deception and dirty tricks are venerable American traditions. For example, in 1800 Thomas Jefferson had to defend himself against the charge that he was dead. Nevertheless, they claim that "our tolerance for absurdity is . . . rising" (p. 4). They compare the American electorate to the Queen in Alice in Wonderland:

> "I can't believe that! said Alice. "Can't you?" the queen said in a pitying tone. "Try again, draw a long breath, and shut your eyes." Alice laughed: "There's no use trying," she said: "one can't believe impossible things." "I daresay you haven't had much practice," said the queen. "When I was younger, I always did it for half an hour a day. Why, sometimes I've believed as many as six impossible things before breakfast." (As quoted in Reeher and Grant, 2004, p. 4.)

Emily Robertson Syracuse University

[1] A version of this chapter, "Teacher Education in a Democratic Society: Learning and Teaching the Practices of Democratic Participation," was published in Marilyn Cochran-Smith, Sharon Feinman-Nemser, and John McIntyre (eds.), *The Handbook of Research on Teacher Education*, 3rd edition, Taylor & Francis, 2008. The author thanks the Taylor & Francis Group, a division of Informa plc, for permission to reproduce portions of that essay in this chapter.

In a similar vein, Matt Miller (2005) asked, in a *New York Times* op-ed piece: "Is it possible in America today to convince anyone of anything he doesn't already believe? If so, are there enough places where this mingling of minds occurs to sustain a democracy?" (p. A15). Miller's question was echoed by Paul Krugman's (2005) complaint that neither politicians nor the electorate are willing to change their views when confronted with decisive contrary evidence. Ideological polarization, the "red" states versus the "blue" states, is evident not only among citizens but also in the House, whose members are often elected from districts created by partisan gerrymandering. Both a gerrymandered House and the niche market media create situations in which people have no need to speak to any but the like-minded (Rosen, 2005; Posner, 2005). Richard Posner (2005) holds that people read newspapers, not to become well informed, but to find "information that will support rather than undermine their existing beliefs" (p. 9).

Confronted with an electorate that seems able to believe "six impossible things before breakfast" and political parties that encourage them to do so, proposals for improving the quality of public political discourse abound. Colleges and universities have gotten into the act. They have been placing greater weight on their civic missions. A few years ago 500 university presidents called upon colleges and universities to help students "realize the values and skills of our democratic society" (as reported in Fish, 2004, n.p.). The Association of American Colleges and Universities has urged its members to consider "What practices provide students with the knowledge and commitments to be socially responsible citizens?" (as reported in Fish, 2004, n.p.). Many colleges and universities include a commitment to civic education within their mission statements. Indeed Robert K. Fullinwider and Judith Lichtenberg (2004) claim that higher education's understanding of the benefits of liberal education has shifted from acquiring liberal culture to preparation for social and civic engagement (Chap. 3).

While a bandwagon may be in motion, not everyone thinks that this is the right direction for higher education to take. For example, Stanley Fish, former Dean of the College of Liberal Arts and Sciences at the University of Illinois at Chicago, has claimed that it is "not the business of the university" to encourage "practices of responsible citizenship . . . in . . . young adults." He holds that the "task would deform (by replacing) the true task of academic work: the search for truth and the dissemination of it through teaching" (Fish, 2004, n.p.).

What are the knowledge, skills, and commitments – the citizen virtues – on which a healthy liberal democracy depends? And what role, if any, should higher education play in developing them? Notice that the question about citizen virtues itself rules out some perspectives on the success of democracy. From the virtue point of view, democracy is not just a matter of having the right institutions, the right political structure, but rather depends on the character of its citizens; hence this view gives political education a fundamental role to play. If democracy is simply a fair system for aggregating and responding to individual citizens' preferences (to consider one alternative view of democracy), civic virtue, and thus civic education, will loom less large. But if democracy tracks justice only if citizens in their deliberations aim at the common good, rather than simply securing their own reasonable interests, for example, care and concern for the common good must be nurtured.

I will argue that the role of citizen in a liberal democracy requires the ability to engage in multiple practices through which citizens codetermine the goods they will pursue together as citizens, and negotiate the differences that divide them. The fact that citizens hold different and conflicting views about how individual and public life should be led, as well about what justice demands, makes these negotiations necessary. The freedom a liberal democratic society provides for voicing differences of opinion and acting on them, within the limits of the law, makes continuous conversation about public matters a requirement of democratic life. The political polarization described earlier represents a failure of engagement in this fundamental democratic task: if there is no "mingling of minds," no willingness to change ones views in the give and take of conversation, no openness to engaging with any but the likeminded, can democracy worthy of the name be sustained? And what role does higher education play in developing the competence of citizens to participate in the practices of democratic life?

8.2 The Civic Sphere and the Practices of Democratic Citizens

The virtues we imagine citizens should possess depend on our conception of political life. What is the political domain, the sphere of civic action? And what actions are called for in that domain? The contexts that come readily to mind when political action is invoked are places where participants are making binding decisions, such as legislatures, courts, and school board meetings. Recently, however, theorists have explored the potential of civil society for democratic action. "Civil society "refers to the social sphere of voluntary associations formed by citizens to express their interests and commitments, associations that are largely outside the spheres of the economy and the state. As Iris Marion Young (2000) says: "In the associations of civil society people co-ordinate their actions by discussing and working things out, rather than by checking prices or looking up the rules" (p. 159). Civil society, in this sense, includes churches, neighborhood associations, workers' organizations, political action groups, clubs, cultural organizations, nonprofit service providers, civic associations, and many others. Such groups may provide services for their members, can expose injustice in the political and economic spheres, and sometimes succeed in placing limits on state and economic power. Young suggests categorizing these associations as private, civic, and political. Although not all associations in civil society are positive (e.g., the Ku Klux Klan), in their civic and political forms, these associations have the potential for strengthening democratic life. The inclusion of civil society in the political domain extends the possibilities for political action beyond the sphere of the state and opens up wider possibilities for democratic participation. The expansion of the political sphere to include civil society mirrors John Dewey's (1966/1916) expansive and inclusive conception of democratic life as "a mode of associated living, of conjoint communicated experience" (p. 87).

Further, Jane Mansbridge (1999) argues for including what she calls "everyday talk" as a potential site for political action. Mansbridge defines as political " 'that which the public ought to discuss' when that discussion forms part of some, perhaps highly informal, version of a collective 'decision' " (p. 214). While legislatures aim at decisions that will be binding on the participants, everyday talk creates the climate of opinion within which binding decisions can be made (or through which such decisions are realized). From this perspective, Mansbridge suggests, "The snort of derision one might give at a sexist television character while watching with friends" is a political act (p. 214).

Without a conception of the politics that involves civil society and everyday talk, many citizens' political activity will consist of voting and being bound by the results. These are important actions, no doubt. And certainly the latter (i.e., the willingness to adhere to the results of a fair election) is a virtue of democratic citizens that is not to be taken for granted. A willingness of citizens to accept the legitimacy of the decisions made and consider themselves bound by them, even when they vehemently disagree, is a part of democratic character. Nevertheless, voting and obeying the law are minimal citizen actions. Including civil society and everyday talk generates a most robust domain for our consideration without supposing that all citizens will have opportunities to be decision-makers in the narrow sense.

What types of actions, what practices, do we engage in as citizens, not only in contexts where decisions are to be made but also in civil society and through everyday talk? And what knowledge, skills, and virtues do these forms of action require? There are many candidates, but in this essay I will consider three categories of citizen practices: (1) deliberation; (2) bargaining and negotiation; and (3) social activism. These practices represent different visions of the work of citizens and their proper orientation to each other. Moreover, these forms of interaction are often in tension with each other, as we shall see. Yet my thesis is that democratic political life requires them all. While some citizens may specialize in one category or another as life stances, most of us engage in all three practices, at least within civil society and everyday talk.

8.2.1 Deliberation

Many of the recent discussions of civic virtue assume that the prime thing citizens ought to do together is deliberate. I have in mind here theories of what is called "deliberative democracy." From this perspective, when confronted with a public problem, citizens try to figure out the best solution to the problem through joint consideration of the reasons for and against proposed courses of action. Alan Wertheimer (1999) says that "In general, we deliberate with each other when we think that (1) there is a right answer to an issue and (2) discussion will move us closer to that answer" (p. 171). Michael Walzer (2004) characterizes deliberation as a way of "reaching decisions through a rational process of discussion among equals, who listen respectfully to each other's views, weigh the available data, consider alternative possibilities, argue about relevance and worthiness, and then choose the best policy for the country or the best person for the office" (p. 91). When citizens deliberate, then, they seek truth or the best course of action through analysis of the available evidence in a process of discussion with fellow participants.

Juries are examples of citizen deliberation. We assume that there is a truth of the matter – the person charged is either guilty or innocent. The jury's task is to assess the evidence and decide on a verdict. We do not think that juries should compromise or "split the difference" when there is disagreement. If the charge is murder in the first degree and some jurors believe that the defendant is guilty while others think he is totally innocent, it would be wrong of them to compromise by convicting him of a lesser charge, say manslaughter. Their task is to agree on the direction the available evidence points to or to acknowledge that they cannot agree on a verdict. A bargain based on mutual interest is not appropriate in cases where the charge is to deliberate.

While deliberation is a familiar activity, it is perhaps not often realized quite how strenuous the ideal is. Deliberation is not merely talking nor is it a debate. As Deborah Tannen (1999/1998) puts the point in her book, *The Argument Culture*, "Public discourse requires *making* an argument for a point of view, not *having* an argument – as in having a fight" (p. 4). In a debate, the opponents are trying to win, not to discover the truth. They may present the evidence that favors their case and not acknowledge the contrary evidence. Debaters are not trying to find the best solution by keeping an open mind about the opponent's point of view. If debate aids truth it is because the members of the audience are led to truly deliberate based on what they have heard (Walzer, 2004). Deliberators, unlike debaters, are open to rational persuasion, to the possibility of being shown wrong.

In a deliberative policymaking process, citizens have the opportunity to respond to proposals made by their representatives and the proposals are amended in light of their comments. Deliberative democrats Amy Gutmann and Dennis Thompson (1996) offer Oregon's efforts in the early 1990s to develop priorities for its Medicaid budget as an example of citizen deliberation. Initially the Oregon Health Services Commission prepared a ranked list of medical conditions based on a cost–benefit analysis. When the list generated a lot of criticism (capping a tooth ranked higher than an appendectomy), the commission solicited citizen input in a variety of ways, including random telephone surveys of citizens' views and numerous community meetings at various locations throughout the state. Groups other than the Commission analyzed the data that was generated. Participants in the town meetings were asked "to think and express themselves in the first person plural . . . as members of a statewide community for whom health care has a shared value" (as quoted in Gutmann and Thompson, 1996, p. 143).

All theories of deliberative democracy attempt to specify the conditions under which such public discussions can be regarded as legitimate (e.g., that all citizens should have an equal and effective right to participate) and they attempt to specify the citizen virtues that are required for successful public debate (e.g., willingness to listen to and seriously entertain other citizens' points of view). The point of the deliberation is to convert disagreement into agreement about what to do by determining which proposals are supported by the best reasons. Deliberative democrats recognize that disagreement may be persistent. Nevertheless, they believe that the mutual respect involved in the process of deliberation will enhance the legitimacy of whatever decision is ultimately made even in the eyes of those who lose out. Losers are expected to feel better because their opinions have been heard. The Oregon example fell short of this ideal in many ways, especially because the proposal restricted access to health care for poor citizens, who did not tend to be represented in the deliberations. Nevertheless, when citizens and the legislature saw what serious restrictions would have to be imposed given the available budget, more money was allocated to the program. Public deliberation did seem to improve the outcome.

If deliberation looms large in public life, then it seems evident that university education will enhance the civic virtue of its graduates, not necessary because higher education aims at civic virtue, but because of its essential role in developing the knowledge, attitudes, and skills required for serious inquiry. By teaching its students how to engage in "the search for truth," as Stanley Fish put it, by teaching them to respect the weight of reasons, to consider alternative points of view, and to be open to being shown wrong universities will help prepare citizens to engage in civic deliberation. They will enhance the quality of public reason.

But is deliberation a frequent component of public political debate? Admittedly, it does not seem to capture the real world very well. If we think about the quality of conversation during recent presidential elections, reasonableness, open-mindedness, and willingness to be shown wrong are not the first adjectives that come to mind. But the model offers an ideal to be aspired to, not a description of reality. To what extent *should* political discussion depend on mutual persuasion about the rightness of particular policies and courses of action? Can political action rightly take other ends? Are these alternatives morally second best to deliberation even if they may be more efficient or expedient? Advocates of deliberation do not generally argue that deliberation is the only acceptable political activity, but they do tend think that it has moral advantages over other activities and is preferred when possible. Is this true?

Dewey (1966/1916) modeled public political discourse as joint inquiry. But others have held that in a *democratic* society, deliberation plays a more limited role. Some believe that the deliberative stance pays too little attention to "the degree to which moral disagreements in politics are shaped by differences of interest and power" (Shapiro, 1999, p. 29). Daniel Bell (1999) argues that if a country is deeply divided between rich and poor and lacks a sense of community and mutual trust, "the solution might be expropriation rather than deliberation" (p.73). The political philosopher Will Kymlicka (2003) suggests that cooperation among diverse groups may be "more a matter of bargaining and negotiation than of genuinely shared deliberation or mutual understanding" (p. 165). Are advocates of deliberation attempting to transcend politics – are they trying to create "a world where political conflict, class struggle, and cultural differences are all replaced by pure deliberation?" asks Walzer (2004, p. 105).

8.2.2 *Bargaining and Negotiation*

Bargains represent the balance of power, not the force of the arguments. The parties trying to reach agreement are seeking to secure their own interests, not necessarily to transcend them through appeal to a common conception of justice or concern for the common good, as the deliberative democrat might want. However, since agreements are more likely to be stable if they give each party a decent measure of satisfaction of their interests, accommodating each other will generally be in the interest of each of the negotiating parties. Wertheimer (1999) says that "We may seek to accommodate each other when we believe that there is no right answer to an issue or that continued deliberation will not likely resolve the dispute (even if there is a right answer)" (p. 171). An accommodation attempts to reach an agreement all can accept. Nevertheless, a mutually agreed to bargain or accommodation may not represent anyone's idea of the best solution, meaning the one that is best supported by the available reasons.

Walzer (2004) claims that "government policy in a democracy is more often the result of a negotiating process . . . than of a deliberative process" (p. 97). Advocates of deliberative democracy are wary of negotiation even as they sometimes acknowledge the need for it. Walter C. Parker (2003), for example, distinguishes negotiation from deliberation by noting that bargaining assumes competing interests and involves "at least two groups present in the same forum engaged in an adversarial contest" (p. 81). Gutmann (2005) says that bargaining is "self-interested or group-interested" – a "politics of manipulation and coercion" rather than "a politics of reasoning and persuasion" (p. 354). And she notes: "Without the capacity to deliberate, there would be no escaping from power politics – which give power priority over both justice and deliberation – which all moral conceptions of democracy are intent on avoiding" (p. 353). Gutmann does acknowledge, however, that bargaining and negotiation might be called for in situations where no moral issue is at stake or at least one party to the dispute is unwilling to take a moral point of view and so those who did so would be disadvantaged.

But is negotiation or bargaining necessarily morally suspect? Strategies for forging agreements among opposing parties obviously vary. A winner takes all power politics, and leaves a few crumbs at best for the loser. Competitive struggles are determined by the balance of power or by force. Yet bargains are required when each side needs the other. If one side can force its will on the others, there is no need to negotiate. Generally, parties in a bargaining or negotiating situation have interdependent interests; they need each other's cooperation to some extent in order to serve their own interests. Each has some power either to reward or to frustrate the other's satisfaction of their needs.

Morton Deutsch's (2000a) theory of negotiation emphasizes this interdepend-ence rather than competitive struggle. From this perspective, constructive conflict resolution requires shifting perspective from conflicts in worldviews or moral prin-ciples (which usually are nonnegotiable) toward the primary interests of the con-flicting parties. What is required is to enlist the parties in a collaborative investigation of how to satisfy the primary interests of each in the specific context. In a sense, this strategy transforms negotiations into deliberation about how to reach an agreement all can accept. Yet the agreement sought is not the objectively right outcome but an arrangement that accommodates each of the parties.

Some of the most difficult conflicts are those where moral principles cannot be set aside because the conflict concerns different interpretations of principles of jus-tice. Deutsch (2000b) offers an example of a mediated conflict resolution where the conflict involved how teacher representatives to a site-based management team should be selected. The issue was whether seats should be designated for teachers from minority groups that were heavily represented among the students but not among the teachers. The school's Black Teacher Caucus held that the management team needed their input, given the diversity of the student body and the importance of the school's dealing with increases in bias-related incidents, and developing a curriculum more relevant to the current student population. The majority of council members held that all members should be elected through democratic procedures and that setting aside a seat for an African-American teacher would open the door to still other seats dedicated to other minority groups. With the help of a mediator, they were ultimately able to agree on a solution that involved the principal's appoint-ing a seven-person multicultural task force each year from which two members of the council would be selected, one at large by vote of the task force and one from the ethnic group most prevalent in the student population (pp. 3–4). The challenge in such cases is to find a creative solution that allows the claims of each side to be represented and the principles that each invokes to be included (Deutsch, 2000a).

Despite the disdain sometimes expressed by deliberative democrats of negotiation as a moral enterprise, democratic citizens arguably need the virtues and skills of conflict resolution that are useful in finding peaceful accommodation of others' inter-ests or creative solutions to conflicts of moral principles. Given the persistence of disagreement among citizens about which policies and practices are best, the attitudes and strategies fostered by training in creative conflict resolution offers a positive alternative to the political polarization we frequently confront. Further, some believe that the danger to democratic politics stems more from the pursuit of truth than from negotiation and compromise. In *The House of Intellect*, Jacques Barzun (1959) argued that "the greatest danger to a democratic state is probably the contamination of its politics by Intellect" (p. 146). He held that the "threat of 'great ideas' to the peaceful conduct of ordinary life is plain: compromise, bargains, tolerance, the salu-tary neglect of trivial acts – all these are at once ruled out. . . . The wars of ideas have always been the most fanatical and needlessly prolonged of all wars" (p. 146).

I confess that I am not entirely clear about what the university's role, if any, is in teaching its students the political arts of bargaining and negotiation. Like all institutions, the university has its own internal politics in which bargaining and mutual accommodation play their roles. And students may engage in such politics in their extracurricular activities. But negotiation and compromise do not, I think, loom large in the curriculum of liberal education, although it may be the focus of some forms of professional education (learning to become a negotiator in labor relations, for example). In courses with service requirements, the point often seems to be to develop greater concern for the public good (which is, of course, valuable) rather than learning to accommodate competing interests.

There are, however, limitations to the scope of constructive conflict resolution. When conflict is generated by injustice, especially injustice that is difficult to recognize by those who perpetrate it because it is embedded within major social institutions, a reorientation of thinking is required, not simply creative solutions. Some citizens must learn to enlarge the scope of their moral communities and recognize their complicity in the persistence of unjust treatment of other citizens. Those who have been unjustly treated are often more likely to recognize their situation and organize to become forces for social change. This work exemplifies the final practice of democratic citizenship surveyed here, activism oriented toward social justice.

8.2.3   Social Activism

While deliberating and bargaining tend to take place within given social structures, activists work to change structures they view as unjust. They attend to differences of power, to the way the context of discussion has been framed by actions outside its scope. The activist believes that deliberation typically occurs in contexts that have been structured in ways that serve the interests of those in power. Thus deliberation is not likely to be effective in securing greater social justice or advancing the interests of the oppressed. Activists employ other strategies of mobilization, protest, and disruption that call attention to their causes. Unlike bargainers, activists are not usually motivated solely by securing their own or even their group's interests. Rather, they see themselves as acting in the interest of more universal principles of justice (Young, 2002). Some citizens make activism their life's work, their profession, in effect. They identify with a social movement and devote themselves to realizing its goals. The civil rights movement, feminist movements, disability rights, gay pride, People for the Ethical Treatment of Animals (PETA), the AIDS Coalition to Unleash Power (ACT UP) are but part of a long list of causes.

Citizens have moments of activism within everyday talk even if it is not a major part of their identities. The following example is taken from Jane Mansbridge's (1999) research. An African-American woman went with her husband to his family's home in the South. At dinner, the men gathered at the table while the women went into the kitchen and came back with plates filled with food for the men. The visiting woman had remained seated at the table. Her husband asked her to fill his plate. She said, "I don't fill your plate at home. Why would I do it here?" And the other women sat down as well and stopped waiting on the men. The woman said, "Well, what I did was I ended up like liberating the other women in the family."

Mansbridge comments: "With this small act – a combination of speech, and, in this case, nonperformance of an expected action – [she] . . . intervened in her own and others' lives to promote a relatively new ideal of gender justice, exemplified by her verb 'liberating' " (pp. 217–218).

Does the university rightly teach students to adopt activist stances? This is a contested question. Stanley Fish (2004) says no because it would require universities to decide "in advance which of the competing views of morality and citizenship is the right one" and then to devote "academic resources and energy to the task of realizing it" (n.p.). On the other hand, the philosopher Richard Rorty (1989) has argued that creating a new vocabulary, a new way of thinking, that enables new practices that challenge injustice in the current system is one activist line of work. And creating new ways of thinking is a primary role of the university. The university is an incubator for social criticism. The institutional autonomy of the university and the academic freedom of faculty members honor the university's mission as social critic.

8.3 Democratic Practices and the Role of Higher Education

A democratic citizen should have the knowledge, skills, and commitments necessary for the various practices required by a democratic life that likely will always be full of contention. Deliberation, negotiation, and activism are core practices in which citizens engage with each other over the issues that divide them. The democratic culture sets the ground rules for engagement: a commitment to the freedom and equality of all citizens (Rawls, 1993). A robust civic education, fueled in part through university education, fosters the democratic culture through preparing future citizens for participation in basic practices of democratic life.

There are both commonalities and tensions among these practices. For example, both deliberation and activism, as I have portrayed them, aim at the common good. In deliberative fora, citizens speak from their own perspectives, of course, but they are expected to be open to rational persuasion about which solution to their common problem is best. Activism that aims at social justice seeks to educate, and appeal to, a conception of the appropriate treatment of persons and the equality of citizens. While redistribution of social goods may advantage some more than others, the reason for the redistribution activists seek is remedying injustice, not responding to special interests.

By contrast, negotiation aims at mutual accommodation of interests and thus has appeared to some to be inferior to the moral stances of deliberation and the demand for social justice. Bargaining is not oriented toward the common good and it is extremely doubtful that a "hidden hand" will see to it that the common good is served by the pursuit of individual and group interests. Yet deliberative democrats acknowledge that agreement is not always forthcoming. Disagreement is a ubiquitous fact of democratic political life. John Rawls (1993) has argued that such disagreement can persist without anyone being ill-informed or mistaken about the facts, because, for example, different groups may assign different weightings to competing values. Joseph M. Schwartz (1995) argues for the "permanence of the political." By that phrase, he means that even in "a relatively egalitarian political community" there will still be "spirited political disagreement and contestation" (p. 19). He suggests that radical democratic theorists have underestimated the persistence of conflict and have supposed that politics as the mediation of conflicting interests could be eliminated in a truly just and egalitarian society. Deliberation and activism share a hope that conflict can be eliminated by seeking truth, whether it is the truth about which policy is best or how justice can be achieved. Negotiation (or "politics" in Schwartz's formulation) acknowledges the radical pluralism of interests and cultural commitments that makes overcoming conflict unlikely except through repression.

While the deliberative forum strives to be a power-free zone, negotiation and activism recognize, in their own ways, the reality of differential distribution of power. Each is willing to use power in pursuit of its goals, unlike the deliberator's focus on rational persuasion. While activism aimed at social justice seeks a redistribution of power, negotiation acknowledges the existing power relationships. Yet constructive negotiation relies on the interdependence of even those with unequal power and the capacity of each party to thwart the interests of the others.

How, then, shall we live together as democratic citizens in the face of continuing disagreement? Should we choose among these practices? Deliberation has much to recommend it even if agreement is not always reached. In public political contexts, voting or the courts may decide the matter for the time being, while deliberation continues. But in civil society or everyday life, beyond the reach of voting and courts, trying to achieve mutual accommodation with others through agreements that satisfy the primary interests of each group seems equally a staple of democratic life. And legislative proposals themselves typically embody bargains based on accommodation of different interests. Lack of willingness to accommodate others, insisting on one's own claim to truth, thwarts legislative action and polarizes the electorate. But when conflict is generated by injustice, especially injustice that is difficult to recognize by those who perpetrate it because it is embedded within major social institutions, a reorientation of thinking is required, not simply creative accommodations of interests. Thus activism oriented to social justice has its distinct claim on democratic life.

Thus it is no surprise that, while I have described each of these political practices independently, in reality, they often appear in combination. For example, a *New York Times*' reporter was struck by the oddity of two ACT UP protesters engaged in a "die-in" while wearing sports jackets and ties. When she followed up, she learned that, after the protest, they were attending a meeting at the office of the United States trade representative (as cited in Levinson, 2002). Activism aimed at changing citizens' awareness of issues is not incompatible with employing deliberative strategies when they are available.

In *Democracy and Disagreement*, deliberative democrats Gutmann and Thompson (1996) consider the example of the strategies used by Senator Carol Moseley Braun to defeat efforts to renew the Daughters of the Confederacy's patent on the Confederate flag insignia. After the amendment passed a test vote, Moseley Braun took to the Senate floor. She argued that putting the Senate's "imprimatur" on a racist symbol was an "outrage" and "insult" that was "absolutely unacceptable" to her and millions of Americans both black and white. Her speech was described as an "oratory of impassioned tears and shouts" and she threatened a filibuster. At the end of a three-hour debate, the amendment failed. Commenting on this example, Gutmann and Thompson (1996) write: "even extreme non-deliberative methods may be justified as necessary steps to deliberation" (p. 135). Yet they also point out that her appeal might not have succeeded if it had been "purely strategic, asserting only a claim of interest and making no appeal to moral principle" (Gutmann and Thompson, 1999, p. 258). That is, if she had made the issue a matter of bargaining or accommodation to ensure the interests of African-Americans as a group, rather than making a moral appeal, based on justice, she would have been less effective. Yet Moseley Braun cannot have been unaware that the interests in reelection of the senators who initially opposed her were part of what made them yield. In this case, deliberation, negotiation, and activism combined to generate a resolution. Choosing among these practices, then, is not only not required, but also not a good idea. Each has its place in the repertoire of a democratic citizen.

The goal of democratic education might be to educate citizens who would realize the following ideals, as represented by Walzer's (2004, pp. 107–108) thought experiments:

> [W]e can imagine the party platform drawn up by a group of people who are not only good negotiators but reflective men and women, who aim at proposals that are morally justified and economically realistic as well as politically appealing. We can imagine a negotiating process in which people try to understand and accommodate the interests of the other side (while still defending their own) rather than just driving the hardest possible bargain. We can imagine parliamentary debates where the rival speakers listen to one another and are prepared to modify their positions. And finally, we can imagine citizens who actually think about the common good when they evaluate candidates, or party programs, or the deals their representatives strike, or the arguments they make.

Of the three types of activities I surveyed, I believe the university contributes most to deliberation and to social criticism that underpins activism, as I have argued. But unlike Stanley Fish, I think that the university aids civic education, not despite its commitment to the search for truth, but because of that commitment. By teaching students the skills of inquiry and respect for truth, including the willingness to change perspectives when confronted with compelling contrary evidence, universities will help prepare citizens to engage in civic deliberation and social criticism. They will enhance the quality of public reason.

But the university's capacity to play the role I have ascribed to it depends on its maintaining what is sometimes called "institutional autonomy." To maintain its position as truth seeker and social critic, the university has to maintain the capacity to speak truth to power whatever the dominant sources of power are at a given historical moment. While contemporary university scholars attack the injustices embedded in our social and political life, universities as institutions are increasingly connected to the agendas of state governments and corporations. Examining the curriculum and the education provided to students is thus only one part of the civic mission of universities. Universities need to examine their own actions as corporate agents for consistency with maintaining the ability to speak truth to power.

A couple of years ago, I attended the Martin Luther King Day dinner at my university. We met in the campus' main athletic facility. It was large event and some people had distant views of the stage and the speaker, so the instant replay screen normally used for athletic events was pressed into service. In the opening moments, old footage of the civil right movement was projected onto the screen, which is surrounded by advertisements for several businesses. I found it a disquieting moment to view images of nonviolent protesters being beaten by the police in juxtaposition with the advertisements. Later the image of our speaker, President Ruth Simmons of Brown University, was on the same screen. As she challenged our students to be less concerned with Hummers and bling-bling and more concerned with social justice, the ads surrounded her face.

That image stayed with me as a metaphor of the moral and political challenges facing contemporary universities. I am not suggesting that it is necessarily wrong for universities to have corporate sponsors for their enterprises. Nor am I saying that business is necessarily a morally contaminated activity from which universities should keep their distance in order to maintain purity. But universities do need to think hard about structuring government and corporate partnerships in ways that do not compromise their essential roles as truth seeker and social critic. Without returning to the idea of the university as an ivory tower, unengaged in the affairs of the community, it is important to maintain institutional autonomy if universities are to fulfill their civic roles. Those roles include preparing their students to participate in deliberative discussions with other citizens and to be attuned to the requirements of social justice.

References

Barzun, J. (1959). *The house of intellect*. New York: Harper Torchbooks of Harper & Row.

Bell, D. A. (1999). Democratic deliberation: The problem of implementation. In S. Macedo (Ed.), *Deliberative politics: Essays on democracy and disagreement* (pp. 70–87). New York: Oxford University Press.

Deutsch, M. (2000a). Cooperation and competition. In M. Deutsch and P. T. Coleman, *The handbook of conflict resolution: Theory and practice* (pp. 21–40). San Francisco: Jossey-Bass.

Deutsch, M. (2000b). Introduction. In M. Deutsch and P. T. Coleman, *The handbook of conflict resolution: Theory and practice* (pp. 1–17). San Francisco: Jossey-Bass.

Dewey, J. (1966/1916). *Democracy and education*. New York: The Free Press.

Fish, S. (2004). Why we built the ivory tower. NYTimes.com. Accessed 21 May 2004 from http://www.nytimes.com/2004/05/21/opinion/21FISH.html?ex = 1086167589&ei = 1&en = 7959c8d2cfff8d1b.

Fullinwider, R. K. & Lichtenberg, J. (2004). *Leveling the playing field: Justice, politics, and college admissions*. Lanham, MD: Rowman & Littlefield.

Gutmann, A. (2005). Afterword: Democratic disagreement and civic education. In S. Fuhrman and M. Lazerson (Eds.), *The public schools* (pp. 347–359). Oxford, England: Oxford University Press.

Gutmann, A. & Thompson, D. (1996). *Democracy and disagreement*. Cambridge, MA: Belknap Press of Harvard University Press.

Gutmann, A. & Thompson, D. (1999). Democratic disagreement. In S. Macedo (Ed.), *Deliberative politics: Essays on democracy and disagreement* (pp. 243–279). New York: Oxford University Press.

Krugman, P. (2005, July 15). Karl Rove's America. *The New York Times*, A19.

Kymlicka, W. (2003). Multicultural states and intercultural citizens. *Theory and Research in Education* 1, 147–169.

Levinson, N. (2002). Deliberative democracy and justice. In S. Rice (Ed.), *Philosophy of education 2001* (pp. 56–59). Urbana, IL: Philosophy of Education Society.

Mansbridge, J. (1999). Everyday talk in the deliberative system. In S. Macedo (Ed.), *Deliberative politics: Essays on democracy and disagreement* (pp. 211–239). New York: Oxford University Press.

Miller, M. (2005, June 4). Is persuasion dead? *The New York Times*, A15.

Parker, W. C. (2003). *Teaching democracy: Unity and diversity in public life*. New York: Teachers College Press.

Posner, R. A. (2005, July 31). Bad news. *The New York Times*, Book Review, 1, 8–11.

Rawls, J. (1993). *Political liberalism*. New York: Columbia University Press.

Reeher, G. and Mero, J. (2004, October 10). Does the truth matter anymore? *The Post Standard*, Section C, 1, 4.

Rorty, R. (1989). *Contingency, irony, and solidarity*. Cambridge: Cambridge University Press.

Rosen, J. (2005, June 12). Center court. *The New York Times* Magazine, Section 6, 17–18.

Schwartz, J. M. (1995). *The permanence of the political: A democratic critique of the radical impulse to transcend politics*. Princeton, NJ: Princeton University Press.

Shapiro, I. (1999). Enough of deliberation: Politics is about interests and power. In S. Macedo (Ed.), *Deliberative politics: Essays on democracy and disagreement* (pp. 28–38). New York: Oxford University Press.

Tannen, D. (1999/1998). *The argument culture*. New York: Ballantine Books.

Walzer, M. (2004). *Politics and passion: Toward a more egalitarian liberalism*. New Haven, CT: Yale University Press.

Wertheimer, A. (1999). Internal disagreements: Deliberation and abortion. In S. Macedo (Ed.), *Deliberative politics: Essays on democracy and disagreement* (pp. 170–183). New York: Oxford University Press.

Young, I. M. (2000). *Inclusion and democracy*. Oxford: Oxford University Press.

Young, I. M. (2002). Activist challenges to deliberative democracy. In S. Rice (Ed.), *Philosophy of education 2001* (pp. 41–55). Urbana, IL: Philosophy of Education Society.

Chapter 9
Love and Hatred in the Moral Life: Educational Investigations

Ann Diller

Abstract How might democratic educators work more fruitfully with such powerful emotions as hatred and love? In a search for answers, this chapter draws upon diverse wisdom traditions as New England poetry, John Dewey's pragmatism, Native American lore, and western as well as eastern Buddhism. This exploration leads to the discovery of suggestive clues for educative possibilities.

> FIRE AND ICE
> Some say the world will end in fire,
> Some say in ice.
> From what I've tasted of desire
> I hold with those who favor fire.
> But if I had to perish twice,
> I think I know enough of hate
> To say that for destruction ice
> Is also great
> And would suffice.
>
> Robert Frost

Numerous violent episodes in recent, and ancient, human history illustrate how the ice of hatred can join with the fires of a desire for vengeance to bring about considerable destruction. Of course, desire comes in different forms; the desire for vengeance is only one, and not usually the first, to spring to mind. When we think of desire, romantic or erotic love springs to mind sooner and carries more pleasant images in its wake. Indeed, we assume the phrase "love and hatred" states a conjunction of polar opposites. Nevertheless, on a superficial level they exhibit striking similarities. Robert Frost's poem evokes some of these parallels.

Love as "desire" resembles hatred insofar as both can feel like powerful uncontrollable forces that take us over – so we "lose ourselves" in them, or we become "not ourselves." For example, we speak of "falling in love," "being obsessed with love," "being madly in love." Romantic love has been portrayed as a form of madness or viewed as temporary insanity. Likewise we speak of "being consumed by hatred," "driven by hatred," "obsessed with revenge."

In any case, love and hatred do run through our lives as human beings in ways that can feel incomprehensible and out of control. If as educators we are serious

Ann Diller
University of New Hampshire

M.S. Katz et al. (eds.) *Education, Democracy, and the Moral Life*
© Springer Science+Business Media, B.V. 2009

about the moral life, then we might well ask: What could help us, and our students, learn to work with the powerful energies we experience as love and hatred?

Before we take up our central question, another preliminary question calls for clarification: What does it mean to take an educational perspective here? In this chapter, to do "educational investigations" means we make these common human experiences of love and hatred an object of direct conscious study in order both (a) to reach a better understanding of the phenomena themselves, and also (b) to consider possibilities for learning how to work with our experiences of love and hatred, keeping in mind our visions of a moral life. Because education is about learning, about learning new things, our investigations are filled with curiosity, with an openness to surprises, and with a willingness to look in unexpected places.

9.1   A Collective, Seductive Misconception: Our War Is the War to End All Wars

Although most of us have experienced or can at least imagine the seductive powers of desire, the parallel powers of hatred may be less accessible to our conscious minds, or direct experience. Yet the attractions and all-embracing obsessive nature of being taken over by forces propelled by hatred may be even stronger, more powerful, and when experienced on a collective level, as in warfare, almost irresistible. In his essay "Nostalgia for the Front," Pierre Teilhard de Chardin's ([1917]/1978) account of his own direct experience conveys some taste of how captivating such a full surrender to the cause of one's war can be.

As a soldier–priest and noncombatant stretcher-bearer, whose task was to rescue the wounded, Pierre Teilhard de Chardin's role at the front, in the French trenches of World War I, was not that of a fighting man; he was not there to kill the enemy. Nevertheless, he does seem to have joined in the widespread belief shared among the Allies that they were participants in the "war to end all wars." He himself writes of "the spiritual grandeur of the battle that is being fought, the triumphant domination of the moral energies released" (p. 175).[1]

Entering a war zone can certainly be akin to entrance into a zone dominated by hatred or by a surrender to the forces of hatred. Thus it could carry parallels to the experiences described by Teilhard ([1917]/1978):

> As soon as the man who is going up the line enters the first communication trench, he drops the burden of social conventions. . . . there is no longer any difference between night and

---

[1] In using the youthful Teilhard's account here, it's crucial to say that nowhere in his letters or writings does one find any indication or intimations of feelings of hatred toward the "enemy" or toward anyone, for that matter. So this cannot be considered as a first-hand account of "hatred" per se; yet, it can I believe give us a sense or flavor of how people committed to their own battles, where hatred does hold sway or fuels their behaviors and sense of purpose, can experience what Teilhard describes as a "triumphant domination" of what they believe to be released "moral energies."

day. All the enslavements and hard and fast divisions of ordinary life collapse like a house of cards. . . . a satisfaction that verges, perhaps, on the irresponsible, . . . goodnight to the comfortable rear-details is not merely a dismissal of regular routine: it symbolizes and heralds a much more intimate enfranchisement, a release from a wrong concern for self and one's own narrow personality. . . . As the rear fades into a more final distance, so the irksome and nagging envelope of small and great worries, of health, of one's family, of success, of the future . . . slides off the soul by itself, like an old coat. The heart grows a new skin. A reality of a higher or more urgent order chases away and scatters the whirling cloud of individual servitudes and cares. (pp. 172–173)

What Teilhard de Chardin along with so many others, those who died in battle as well as those who survived the "Great War" to "end all wars," could not foresee when he wrote this essay in 1917 was that not only did World War I not live up to its billing to be the "war to end all wars," but that only two decades later Europe would be on the brink of another longer, "greater," and more devastating war. Similar cycles throughout human history lead most moral and spiritual traditions to make a sharp distinction between the energies of love and of hatred.

9.2   An Alternative Vision: Wise Love Heals Hatred

Upon reflection, as well as intuitively, we recognize that love, in its broader sense and in most of its manifestations, follows a radically different path from hatred. In fact, the world's wisdom traditions mark the difference between love and hatred as a profound and significant distinction. For example, the *Dhammapada*, an ancient Buddhist text, contains these lines (in Kornfield 1993, p. 297):

Hatred never ceases by hatred

but by love alone is healed.

This is an ancient and eternal law.

This famous verse from the *Dhammapada* makes two remarkable claims:

1. Hatred never ceases by hatred.
2. Hatred by love alone is healed.

Most students of human history would probably acknowledge we have a preponderance of evidence, accumulated over centuries, to support the first claim that "hatred never ceases by hatred." But the second claim that "Hatred by love alone is healed" seems less obvious, and for my purposes in this essay more intriguing, perplexing, and, perhaps, promising as an arena for educational investigation.

For instance, it is not as if we can simply make a decision to replace hatred with love and presto all is well. As we already noted, what we take to be love, when it is tied to desire can over time, in some cases over a very short period of time, turn from something that looks and feels like love into something that looks and feels like hatred. Thus, not just any sort of "love" will do here if we are looking for a love capable of healing hatred.

Since the claim "Hatred never ceases by hatred, but by love alone is healed" comes from an ancient Buddhist text, it makes sense to assume Buddhist traditions might have something more to say about a love that can heal hatred. And, indeed they do – especially under the aegis of what are called the Brahmaviharas, described by Buddhist scholars as four interdependent aspects of "true love." The common renderings of these into English are: loving-kindness, compassion, sympathetic joy, and equanimity. Together these comprise the "Brahmaviharas" (literally "Sublime Abodes"), also known as "The Four Immeasurables" because it is said these qualities of love can "grow" together into a "boundless love for all living beings" which is "limitless" (i.e., immeasurable) in its "flow outward through the universe."

As we contemplate this "sublime realm" of the "Four Immeasurables" we may begin to imagine hatred could be healed.[2] But what if, at the moment, we feel entrenched in our experiences of hatred? What if we find ourselves mired in hatred, unable to access any of the four elements contained in healing love? Under these circumstances, rather than passively allowing ourselves to remain subjugated, pushed around, and controlled by the forces of hatred, we can undertake an educational investigation into this phenomenon of hatred.

9.3   An Educational Hypothesis: Self-Hatred Holds the Key

If we find ourselves mired in hatred, unable to access any remnants of loving-kindness, compassion, sympathetic joy, or equanimity, then to do an educational investigation means we now take this phenomenon of hatred itself as the object of study. We acknowledge that hatred does hold us captive at the moment; and it leaves us feeling cut off from all forms of healing love. Let us, therefore, look more closely at some salient aspects of the phenomenon of human hatred.

As human beings our inherited nature seems to carry capacities and impulses associated with hatred. These impulses and reactions can operate, or at least get generated, below the level of conscious awareness. In fact, one dangerous, albeit well-intentioned, "moral" method here (also able to operate unconsciously) leads us to repress our feelings of hatred, and/or its associates. Repression enables us to separate our conscious awareness from these presumed-to-be-unacceptable feelings. We may thus avoid facing our own disapproval; we may even delude ourselves into believing these repressed feelings do not affect us in any way, or "do not exist." But, as modern psychology tells us, "what we resist, persists"; and refusing to acknowledge what we feel tends to increase rather than diminish its force. Thus, we get such phenomena as "indirect acting out" or other seemingly inexplicable emotional "explosions."

---

[2]For more detailed discussions of the four Brahamaviharas, see Diller (2004) and Thich Nhat Hahn (1998, pp. 1–9).

In addition to the well-known dangers associated with forms of repression, being alienated from one's most powerful feelings also means being alienated from one's own energy. Yet, if we neither repress nor express hatred, as in the forms of destructive "acting out," what then? Fortunately this is not a new human problem; let us look, therefore, at some standard educational advice. John Dewey (1938) summarizes the key moves when he writes:

> Natural impulses and desires constitute in any case the starting point. But there is no intellectual growth without some reconstruction, some remaking, of impulses and desires in the form in which they first show themselves. This remaking involves inhibition of impulse in its first estate . . . "stop and think" . . . is thus a postponement of immediate action, while it effects internal control of impulse through a union of observation and memory, this union being the heart of reflection. (p. 64).

In summary, following Dewey, we do want to become fully cognizant of our internal impulses, but we also want to "stop" or "inhibit" any "immediate manifestation of impulse" (i.e., any actions or reactions). Instead of moving into some reactive behavior pattern, we pause and give ourselves time to observe our impulses and reflect upon them.

What might we learn about our feelings of hatred, if we "stop" in order to observe and reflect? One preliminary observation reminds us to distinguish between hatred and anger. Frost's "Fire and Ice" poem names the crucial characteristic attribute – hatred resembles ice, hatred is cold. Anger tends to be hot and quickly discharged, while hatred tends to be cold and prolonged. Anger does not normally cut off relationships. In contrast to anger, hatred's coldness keeps us at a distance, separated from those whom we hate.

If we delve into hatred, we encounter a vindictive attitude. Hatred calls for vengeance, for revenge against those who we believe have hurt us. Hatred often carries a calculating deliberate intention to harm those one hates, even to annihilate or obliterate them altogether. As long as we are caught in hatred's belief system, the supposed "solution" cycles us back into another repetition, in some form, of the war to end all wars, either at a personal or a collective level.

Remembering that these are educational investigations characterized by open curiosity and a willingness to look in unexpected places, what about the wisdom traditions that advise us to turn our attention inward? For example, Sangharakshita (1998), a Buddhist author, agrees with our observation about the prevalence of vindictiveness in experiences of hatred. He writes: "As a vindictive attitude – he's done you down and you want to get even by doing him down." Sangharakshita also introduces a further possibility. He suggests one's self-image may be at stake: "hatred has a lot to do with … a subtle sense of one's having been diminished in the eyes of others" (p. 165). Sangharakshita notes that this sense of "having been diminished" could be a "subtle" one, thus not easily seen or acknowledged.

If the sense of self-diminishment has been sufficiently subtle, then one will be more conscious of the externally directed hatred, than of its internal concomitants. In order to explore this further we need to ask: But what makes it possible for us to feel "diminished in the eyes of others?" Is it because the self-image that feels diminished, or threatened, is already precarious? If so, is it precarious because one's sense of self-worth is constantly under inner attack from self-criticism and self-judgment?

Another author states the point more boldly. A. H. Almaas (2003) claims: "Hatred for others cannot exist apart from inner hatred. … There cannot be 'pure hatred' without inner self-directed self-attack." Almaas's account of how inner self-hatred operates helps to highlight its subtlety and to explain why we might not recognize it as such. He says: "When we become aware of the obsessive, frenetic, agitated quality of our inner activity, of our mental movements, we can recognize one of the central energies that powers these activities, namely the obsessive power of self-hatred, which is criticizing, judging, and attacking." Almaas believes self-criticism "arises from an underlying self-hatred, which is an inner, hidden self-hatred that hurts and divides us inside, with a heartless disregard for how we feel" (Personal Lecture Notes, July 30, 2003).

If, upon reflection and investigation, we do discover our internal self-hatred, what then? Does this inward turn afford us a better chance of access to the aspects of healing love? I am inclined to answer: possibly, but not necessarily. In some cases, if we become aware of the existence of self-hatred and of how, as Almaas says, "hidden self-hatred hurts and divides us," our new awareness carries the potential to undermine the hitherto unconscious influence self-hatred derived from its covert operations. In other cases, if we have had difficulty experiencing loving-kindness, compassion, sympathetic joy, and/or equanimity in relation to our hatred of others, we may be just as stuck again in trying to bring them to bear toward our own self-hatred. Indeed, some of us might find this even more difficult.

So even though we have made some progress in our investigations by turning inward, it may not be sufficient to access the love that heals hatred. What do we do? There is a story that might be of use to us at this juncture. Educational lessons occur in stories as easily as in lectures.

9.4 A Teaching Story: The First-Nation Grandfather's Two Wolves

The Story:

> An old First Nation Grandfather said to his grandson who came to him with anger at a friend who had done him an injustice…

> "Let me tell you a story. I too, at times, have felt a great hate for those that have taken so much, with no sorrow for what they do. But hate wears you down, and does not hurt your enemy. It is like taking poison and wishing your enemy would die. I have struggled with these feelings many times."

He continued:

> "It is as if there are two wolves inside me. One is good and does no harm. He lives in harmony with all around him and does not take offense when no offense was intended. He will only fight when it is right to do so, and in the right way.…

> "But the other wolf, ahh! He is full of hate. The littlest thing will set him into a fit of temper. He fights everyone, all the time, for no reason. He cannot think because his anger and hate are so great.…

"Sometimes it is hard to live with these two wolves inside me, for both of them try to dominate my spirit."

The boy looked intently into his Grandfather's eyes and asked: "Which one wins, Grandfather?"

The Grandfather smiled and quietly said: "The one I feed."[3]

As a teaching story, this simple Grandfather's tale carries a number of pertinent points. It demonstrates: (a) an honest acknowledgement of our natural human feelings of "great hate" toward those who have harmed us; (b) a recognition of the internal costs, akin to self-hatred ("like taking poison"); (c) a respect for how powerful and how persistent these feelings can be; and (d) a framework that can accept the repeated experiences of having these feelings of hatred arising, without identifying with them, without repressing them, and without reacting according to their dictates. In addition, the story provides a vital clue for working with our feelings of hatred (as well as with other feelings): (e) it identifies the one place where we can make a conscious choice: we can decide which internal "wolves" we "feed." Let me expand on some of these points by discussing my reading of the story.

The Grandfather recognizes and accepts, in a matter-of-fact way, that powerful persistent feelings of hatred do dwell and arise within him. But he also makes it clear that that these feelings are not who he takes himself to be: they are "two wolves inside me." Taking his perspective we could say that however many "internal wolves" we may, at times, be forced to recognize and acknowledge, we need not be identified with any of them.

The personal space created by this perspective allows for the insights, or partial truths, found in the conventional "permissive" and "repressive" approaches, without being propelled into their distortions or tumbling into their pitfalls. For instance, the conventional *permissive* approach accepts that such feelings as hatred do arise naturally as part of the human condition and thus need to be consciously acknowledged; but it then assumes that we must or can "discharge" these feelings without regard for their possibly harmful consequences. A *repressive* approach, in contrast to a permissive one, does worry about the possibility of harmful consequences from "natural" behavioral discharges, but then assumes it is best therefore to "repress" or at least "suppress" not only the impulsive behaviors, but also the feelings themselves.

Recognition of the feelings without identification with them opens up the spaciousness that can accept the fact that there are internal wolves where I live. In one sense they are a part of me (not to be denied or repressed), and yet in another sense I am much larger, there is considerably more in my environment besides the wolves of hatred.

The Grandfather's image of internal wolves conveys what a powerful life of their own our feelings and emotions display. They do appear like wild animals that emerge suddenly from the depths of the forest and threaten to take us over. As the

---

[3] Author unknown, this story was originally given to me by a native Canadian storyteller, since then various versions have shown up on the Internet. The text in this chapter reflects my own editing.

Grandfather says, "they try to dominate my spirit." But they only "try" to dominate; they do not succeed, because one choice point still exists in these scenarios. The choice point cannot, however, be found at the juncture of determining whether or not such feelings will arise, since these feelings just show up without our bidding. The story concludes by telling us where to find it. It comes at the point of determining what gets fed. The grandfather makes this clear: even though these "wolves" keep appearing, he is not left helpless because he can still decide which wolves he will "feed."

As we follow this tale to the end, it brings us back around to the question of "feeding": which of our internal impulses, and "arisings" will we feed? Which feelings and capacities will we encourage to grow and flourish? If we want to feed and nourish the forms of love that heal hatred, how can this happen? Where do we find such nourishment? To pursue these questions, I want to turn now to a "teaching poem."

9.5   A Teaching Poem: Dust of Snow

If we want to feed and nourish the forms of love that can heal hatred, then, on my reading, another poem from Robert Frost, *Dust of Snow* with its succinct poetic imagery, helps to point the way.

> The way a crow
> Shook down on me
> The dust of snow
> From a hemlock tree
> Has given my heart
> A change of mood
> And saved some part
> Of a day I had rued.

Let us consider some of the implications for our questions about feeding and proper nourishment that might be gleaned from Frost's poetic rendering of how this brief episode with a crow gave his heart a change of mood. It seems to me to contain, at least in its subtext, useful applicable wisdom. I take its central theme to be about *Connection*. In a sense, it might also be Robert Frost's echoing response to Rainer Maria Rilke's verse (in Mitchell 1995, p. 191):

> Ah, not to be cut off,
> not through the slightest partition
> shut out from the law of the stars.
> The inner – what is it?
> if not intensified sky,
> Hurled through with birds and deep
> with the winds of homecoming.

In addition to these poems from Frost and Rilke, a prose passage from the Zen Master and poet Thich Nhat Hanh (1987) speaks to our investigations in this section. These are the opening lines in his book *Being Peace*: "Life is filled with suffering, but it is also filled with many wonders, like the blue sky, the sunshine, the eyes of a baby. To suffer is not enough. We must also be in touch with the wonders of life. They are within us and all around us, everywhere, any time" (p. 3).

When we ask what we need to feed. Certainly our need for connection comes to the forefront. Based on her work assisting people to recover from their experiences of trauma, Judith Lewis Herman (1992) has this to say: "Traumatic events destroy the sustaining bonds between the individual and community. Those who have survived learn that their sense of self, of worth, of humanity, depends upon a feeling of connection to others. The solidarity of a group provides the strongest protection against terror and despair, and the strongest antidote to traumatic experience" (p. 295).

Even though the recognition of our need for connections, whether we have been traumatized or not, is a crucial insight, a further question still remains, namely: Which connections do we feed? Are some connections more likely than others to bring us in touch with the love that heals hatred? If we reconsider our earlier example from Teilhard de Chardin's account of his experiences during World War I, we can see how his reflections fit with Judith Herman's observations about the importance of sustaining "a feeling of connection to others." But, as we saw in the history that followed World War I, if the "solidarity of a group" depends upon other "others" being viewed as "enemies," opposed to, perhaps hated by one's own group, then the cycle of collective hatred still gets perpetuated and even fueled by these very same feelings of connection and solidarity. Yes, connection is crucial, but our connections need to move beyond the bounds of any narrow, exclusive solidarity. Where does this take us?

If we revisit the passages quoted at the beginning of this section, we will, I believe, begin to find our answer. For example, Hanh (1987) speaks of our need for connection as being "in touch with the wonders of life." These "wonders of life" do, of course, include other people ("eyes of a baby"); but they also encompass "the blue sky [and] the sunshine." Rilke too invokes the sky as well as the stars, birds, and winds. For Frost the bird is a crow that bursts in along with the wonders of snow and hemlock trees.

It can be a useful reminder as well as a relief to remember that we can access our sense of connectedness through the natural world – animals, plants, sky, clouds, mountains, rivers, rain, snow, sunshine – particularly at times when we're feeling "cut off" from other people due to troubled or even hateful relationships. It may be easier to restore our feelings of connection if we start with the world of nature. Plants and animals are full of life, but they don't "talk back"; and they never judge or criticize us. This allows us to be less defended, less on guard, thus more able to stay open to surprises, and attend to the details of our present moment awareness.

Indeed, if we can be fully attentive to the details of our present moment awareness, we will feel a restoration of connectedness and we might begin to notice that we already are, and always have been, interconnected. We cannot be other than an integral part of the whole living, dynamic network of the earth, the galaxy, the universe. Hanh introduces the term "interbeing" to describe this truth of our interconnected, interdependent existence. He tells us that the term comes "from the *Avatamsaka Sutra*. . . . In the sutra it is a compound term which means 'mutual' and 'to be.'" When Hanh (1987) first introduced the term "interbeing" in North

America, he said: "Interbeing is a new word in English, and I hope it will be accepted. We have talked about the many in the one, and the one containing the many. In one sheet of paper, we see everything else, the cloud, the forest, the logger. ... That is the meaning of the word 'interbeing'" (p. 87).

If we pause to reflect on what Hanh calls our interbeing and we observe how extensive and unavoidable our interdependence actually is, then we can see clearly how even though at times we may *feel* cut off and *believe* ourselves to be separate, as a matter of fact we never are and cannot be so. Thus, it may become clear to us that any hatred whatsoever directed toward anyone, self, or others, individuals or collectives, will inevitably "pollute" our larger relational field, akin to fueling radiating circles of hatred. Once we see this clearly, it can bring us back to the love that heals hatred.

Let us return to *Dust of Snow* with the concept of interbeing in mind. When we do so, we see that this poem gives us a vivid everyday example of how we can suddenly become aware of, and delight in, our "interbeing" with Nature. For Robert Frost that day it was the natural world in the forms of crow, hemlock tree, and snow. Frost's poem captures the curative, and restorative, effect these reminders of our interbeing can have for us. It illustrates certain truths about the human experience of "moods" that have direct bearing on our search for healing love, in particular with respect to the two aspects of sympathetic joy and even-mindedness, or equanimity.

In reading the poet's playful rhymes about that crow, it is fairly easy to detect a close kinship to sympathetic joy, which is one aspect of the love that heals. Indeed the lighthearted rhythmical feeling of delight in the crow and in his "dust of snow" almost creates healing in the very reading of it. Just as some of us find it easier to restore our sense of connection via the nonhuman world of nature, similarly at times our most accessible experiences of sympathetic joy occur in interactions with a beloved animal, or the intimacy of up-close bird-watching, or being stopped in our tracks by an exuberant freshly blooming flower.

Thus, *Dust of Snow* reminds us of how, even at those times when we feel mired in self-hatred, alienated from feelings of compassion or loving-kindness toward ourselves or any human being, it can still happen that we suddenly stumble into a moment of sympathetic joy upon encountering another creature. The poem also conveys how sensitive our ups and downs can be to external events, to unpredictable encounters. It shows the potentially ephemeral impermanent nature of moods. Here is a place where the perspective of equanimity, or even-mindedness, another aspect of healing love, can enter.

Let us return to our earlier example from Sangharakshita (1998) of being insulted by someone and feeling "he's done you down, and you want to get even by doing him down." Sangharakshita suggests that a shift of perspective to even-mindedness can change these feelings. Here's his description of what you might say to yourself: "'Well, he just lost his temper. He said some foolish things, but in the end it's his problem, not mine.' If you take that attitude, you won't feel put down, and you won't need to get even – because you feel 'even' anyway. Your evenness has not been disturbed" (p. 165).

Sangharakshita's example is an apt one insofar as it calls up those moments of equanimity that do occur sometimes, when it appears obvious to all concerned that another person's insulting behavior toward us reflects no more than that person's own "loss of temper"; and it is clearly about them, not about us. But what of other times when our evenness has been disturbed, when some sense, subtle or not so subtle, of personal diminishment comes over us? In these instances we might recognize the reasonableness of an even-minded perspective, but still feel "put down"? If we are honest with ourselves we cannot deny that, even though it is unwarranted, we nevertheless do feel hurt, perhaps even humiliated.

Sangharakshita's example thus raises questions about how we distinguish between recognizing and not resisting the spontaneous arising of particular feelings, on the one hand, compared with "feeding" them through our beliefs, headlines, narratives, or investment in them, on the other hand. These can be subtle distinctions to sustain, even for mature reflective adults. How do we avoid "feeding" those incipient feelings that threaten to grow into full-blown vindictiveness and/or self-hatred? When we are unable to sustain a larger perspective of equanimity or even-mindedness, then to some extent, on some level, there is the danger that a part of us believes in the stories that "feed" hatred. How can we both acknowledge that this is the case and also give compassionate understanding to the feelings of self-diminishment, without total identification with them?

It seems to me that our best and last resort has to be that of finding ways to bring compassion and loving-kindness to bear on our feelings of self-diminishment. Indeed, Cheri Huber, a contemporary Zen Buddhist teacher considers the clear presence of loving-kindness and compassion to be the best test and antidote to use against the voices of self-hatred. In a discussion reminiscent of Almaas's descriptions of the "obsessive power of self-hatred, which is criticizing, judging, and attacking," Huber (1993) details some of the common "self-improvement" disguises under which self-hatred often manifests itself in our lives. She then gives a succinct summary of her basic principle: "I can give you the simplest of all possible rules of thumb: Any time a voice is talking to you that is not talking with love and compassion, DON'T BELIEVE IT!" Huber continues by noting the connection between self-hatred and externally directed hatred: "Even if it's talking about someone else, don't believe it. Even if it is directed at someone else, it is the voice of your self-hate. It is simply hating you through an external object" (p. 45).

If one can follow up on Huber's recommendations, then loving-kindness and compassion would be brought to bear toward oneself and toward the feelings, content, and circumstances of one's self-hatred. Compassion, sympathy, loving-kindness, and understanding can be directed toward our own pain, toward our discomfort, our experiences of suffering, of sorrow, of feeling diminished, wronged, and oppressed. There could be an active conscious "quivering of the heart" in response to the painful circumstances of hardship and/or helplessness as well as toward the feelings these arouse, such as frustration, powerlessness, anger, hatred, desire for revenge, compulsions to "fight back" in order to harm, or defeat those one deems responsible for the present injuries.

If one can invoke love and compassion on behalf of the pain of his or her self-hatred, then some sympathetic understanding toward one's natural human feelings does seem (at least theoretically) possible. Being compassionate toward but no longer unconsciously identified with the now recognized and exposed self-hatred might in turn free one from its externally directed corollaries. For those of us who tend to be very self-critical, it may be easier to move toward compassion if we start by first reaching out to understand and empathize with the sorrows of others. Just as sympathetic joy often connects us to the diverse manifestations of life in the worlds of nature and of nonhuman creatures, at other times it is someone's pain, suffering, or sorrow that brings forth in us an empathic response.

Yet to access the love that can heal hatred it is necessary to join compassion with equanimity and understanding. For example, in his discussions on the incredibly challenging tasks of mediation and reconciliation between major political blocs, Hanh (1987) calls for people who can "get in touch with both sides, understanding the suffering of each, and telling each side about the other" (p.72). He says that to understand and to describe the suffering being endured by each side will in itself "be a great help for peace" (p.70). In fact, Hanh (1998) is clear and unequivocal in his insistence that all four aspects are interdependent: "For love to be true *love*, it must contain compassion, joy, and equanimity in it. For compassion to be true *compassion*, it has to have love, joy, and equanimity in it. True *joy* has to contain love, compassion, and equanimity. And true *equanimity* has to have love, compassion, and joy in it" (p. 9, my italics).

If we want to access the love that heals hatred, we not only need to understand these complexities, we also need to learn how to nourish our own and each other's capacities for even-mindedness, for sympathetic joy, for compassion, and for loving-kindness. Thus, to achieve any lasting change or transformation requires ongoing "practices." This seems to me particularly necessary when we endeavor to work with those impulses and "passions" such as love and hatred that belong to some of the most primitive ancient regions of human nature. An educational approach would therefore be one that recognizes this need for ongoing, deliberate conscious attention to which "wolves" we are feeding, over and over and over again.

To summarize, our educational investigations have led us to the recognition that there is much complexity and few if any easy answers in working with our human propensities around love and hatred. Nevertheless we have also seen that pausing and looking more deeply at these phenomena does allow us to explore their underpinnings in what are often unconscious self-perpetuating patterns and propensities. In doing so, we can recognize and acknowledge the feelings and impulses thus uncovered. We can learn the importance of questioning ourselves about which "wolves" we happen to be feeding. We can practice "holding" rather than "acting out" the impulses that show up and threaten to fuel our fires of desire. And we can provide the same nonreactive compassionate holding for the wounds, hurts, and feelings of self-diminishment that might otherwise freeze our hearts and leave us prone to hatred's icy cold calculations of revenge. Instead of feeding the destructive powers of fire and ice, we can turn to the feeding and nurturing of our own inherent capacities for loving-kindness, compassion, sympathetic joy, and even-mindedness, that together give us the promise of a love that can heal hatred.

References

Almaas, A. H. (2003, July). Ridhwan Summer Institute, Sacramento, CA. Personal Lecture Notes.

Dewey, J. (1938). *Experience and education*. New York: Macmillan.

Diller, A. (2004). The search for wise love in education: What can we learn from the Brahmaviharas? In D. Liston & J. Garrison (Eds.), *Teaching, learning, and loving* (pp. 169–198). New York: Routledge Falmer.

Frost, R. (1969). *The poetry of Robert Frost: The collected poems, complete and unabridged*. Ed. by E.C. Lathem. New York: Holt, Rinehart & Winston.

Hanh, T. N. (1987). *Being peace*. Berkeley, CA: Parallax Press.

Hanh, T. N. (1998). *Teachings on love*. Berkeley, CA: Parallax Press.

Herman, J. L. (1992). *Trauma and recovery*. New York: Basic Books. Quoted in M. Greenspan, *Healing through the dark emotions*. Boston and London: Shambala, 2004, p. 295.

Huber, C. (1993). *There is nothing wrong with you*. Mountain View, CA: Keep It Simple Books.

Kornfield, J. (1993). *A path with heart*. New York: Bantam.

Mitchell, S. (Ed.). (1995). Ah, not to be cut off. In *Ahead of all parting: The selected poetry and prose of Rainer Maria Rilke* (p. 191). New York: Modern Library.

Sangharakshita. (1998). *Know your mind*. Birmingham, England: Windhorse Publications.

Teilhard de Chardin, P. ([1917]/1978). Nostalgia for the front. In *The heart of matter*. Translated by René Hague. New York and London: Harcourt Brace Jovanovich (pp. 167–181).

Index

Printed in Great Britain
by Amazon.co.uk, Ltd.,
Marston Gate.